Praise for *Home Baked*

"Many books capture the romance of baking, while others convey the nuts and bolts—but rarely does one book hit both chords at the same time. With *Home Baked*, Hanne Risgaard has written a practical, beautiful, and, most importantly, inspiring bread book for the ages. Every page, every recipe, makes me want to gather the grain with my own hands and transform it into earthy, delicious, and gorgeous loaves of bread."
    —Peter Reinhart, author of *Whole Grain Breads* and *Artisan Breads Every Day*

"When I first became a baker, I made a career-changing visit to an organic wheatfield and mill. As a baker I thought I knew flour, but it wasn't until I stood in a wheatfield that I realized that my passion for bread was part of a larger story. *Home Baked* is a testament to the craft that I have enjoyed since 1983. Refreshingly told from the perspective of the miller, the recipes are true to their Nordic origins and never step too far away from the fields on which the grain is grown."
    —Daniel Leader, coauthor of *Bread Alone* and *Simply Great Breads*

"*Home Baked* is an absolute treasure! Plus, its timing couldn't be better with more people (myself included) exploring flours other than modern commercial wheat. I think people will like cooking by weight rather than volume—it will do so much to ensure success in making Hanne Risgaard's straightforward, mouthwatering, and very promising recipes."
    —Deborah Madison, author of *Local Flavors*

"Hanne Risgaard's connection to and understanding of the grains grown and milled on her land at Skærtoft shine through in this beautiful collection of Nordic recipes, drawn from the rich baking heritage of northern Europe. *Home Baked* is atmospheric and appealing!"
    —Richard Bertinet, author of *Dough: Simple Contemporary Breads*

Hanne Risgaard

HOME BAKED

Nordic Recipes and Techniques for Organic Bread and Pastry

Foreword by Jeffrey Hamelman

Photography by Thomas Tolstrup

Translated by Marie-Louise Risgaard,
with Robert Jonathan Whittle

Chelsea Green Publishing
White River Junction, Vermont

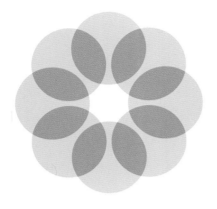

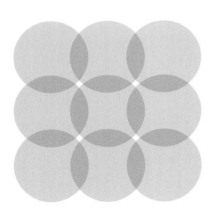

For Bertram, Mille Kirstine, and Albert

"If only it had been a grain of barley,"
sighed the hungry hen,
when she found a diamond in the dung-pile.
Old Danish proverb

Foreword

In Vermont at the beginning of March, 2011, at the annual conference of the Northern Grain Growers Association, I received a delightful gift from a delightful woman—*Hjemmebagt*. The book—a Danish bread book for home bakers—was given to me by Marie-Louise Risgaard and written by her mother, Hanne. In spite of the glossary of baking terms that Marie-Louise patiently wrote out for me in Danish with English translations, I found the language strange to my American eyes, and daunting, so all I did was browse the contents and enjoy the many evocative photographs.

One year later, Marie-Louise contacted me and asked if I'd be willing to write the foreword to the English translation of Hanne's book, now accessibly titled *Home Baked* and scheduled for publication by the venerable and forward-looking Chelsea Green Publishing Company. Based on my enjoyment of the attractive photos of the breads in the Danish version, and my admiration for Marie-Louise, I was happy to consent to her request.

When the manuscript arrived, however, I was a bit tentative; after decades as a professional baker, would I find enough value in a book for home bakers to be able to write a credible foreword? It didn't take many pages of reading before I felt that Hanne was gently tugging me by the shirtsleeve and leading me toward the kitchen. She had already captivated me by her alluring and poetic spirit: who can be unmoved by words such as these from the Preface: *"A summer morning. Early, and already mild. Soft, low light over the field. Green ears of rye, delicately touched with violet."* Once in the kitchen, trying out some of the breads, I felt re-connected to my earliest days of baking at home, enjoying Hanne's direct and unfussy approach. The breads were simple, in the best sense of the word; rather than reading a hundred pages of technical science, you could get out your scale, get out your ingredients, and have breathing dough in half an hour. There's a place for all that science and technical matter, and many avid bakers eventually arrive there and their baking skills become broader and deeper as their academic understanding of bread grows. And there's a place, too, for books that take you right to the end product—come on, let's just make some bread! We don't even need a mixer—we've got hands! This is one way that Hanne's book shines, but there's something even better. The honest integrity of her ingredients, her clear and abiding concern and commitment for human health, and her dedication to environmental cleanliness are as genuine as they are reassuring.

Something else that stands out in *Home Baked* is what, to North American bakers, will seem to be an unusual pairing of ingredients in the breads. Breads with beer or carrots or flower petals, others with nettles or pears, and all the seeded breads, and all the robust organic grains—barley and spelt, wheat and rye—these hearty and vigorous ingredients must suit the climate well, I thought. Reading Hanne's description of the "huge old walnut tree in the garden," and the great August harvests, and the aquavit she makes with the nuts, and the breads, and the competition from those crows—it made me want to book a flight just to see the tree.

I kept finding more and more to enjoy in the book—for instance, all the recipes that come from friends and neighbors, and the stories associated with them; together, they impart a feeling of an intact cultural fabric, with bread as an essential part of the warp and weft of the community. Even without the photographs, the book would be commendable as text alone; but the photos, particularly those of the trees and flowers and the grains in the fields, elevate the book to a greater height, with their vibrant articulation of the visual realm.

Above all, it was the chapter entitled "Leftovers," appropriately placed at the end, that moved me most. Coincidentally, as I was reading the manuscript, I heard a radio report stating that 14 percent of all Vermont households are food-insecure, and that there are 280 hunger-relief agencies in this small state that is my welcome home. One in seven families without enough food in a rural and agricultural state, how could that be? How much hunger, I wondered, could be alleviated just by repurposing the old bread that the crows are picking at in the dumps? What do we do with the inevitable old bread? Feeding the chickens and pigs is great, so is composting it or, as we do in winter, getting some last BTUs out of it by adding it to the wood stove. But first of all, let's feed the humans, and Hanne gives us many ways to do so. When I read the recipe for Rye Bread Porridge with Whipped Cream, I put down the manuscript, went directly to the kitchen, and began cubing old 100% rye bread so I could make it. The diverse recipes in this chapter are not based just on economy, which is in itself amply admirable, they are based on a respect for the earth's resources and the commitment to nourish and not to squander. Hanne underscores the consciousness that characterized humanity for millennia to save and savor every scrap of food.

Home Baked is a book to enjoy, not just for the recipes, but also for Hanne's creativity, diversity, and playful style. She clearly and dearly loves her bountiful grains in all their varied guises, and more than anything wants to impart that love to her readers. Let her take you, too, gently by the shirtsleeve; you will enjoy the fragrances and the conversation.

Jeffrey Hamelman
Hartland, Vermont

A Few Notes
Before Getting Started

The recipes in this book are all based on the use of organic, untreated, stone-ground flour. Whether it's for bread or pastry, stone-ground it is. By "untreated" we mean that we do not add any food additives to our flour, such as improving, oxidizing, or reducing agents—not even ascorbic acid, which is allowed by the organic standards. To achieve the highest quality possible, we always take great care to use only the best grains, and we never mix individual loads. The result is single-field traceability along with an uncompromising high quality level.

At Skærtoft Mølle we do not use our stone mill for making whole-grain flour alone. We also make "high-extraction" flour; that is, we sift, or bolt, our whole-grain flour at 200 μm (microns) to take out the coarser bran particles, thus ending up with an extraction rate of 80 to 85 percent. This is *our* version of "white" flour. We very proudly ensure that the fine bran particles and the germ are retained in it, although we know that when you are using this type of flour your bread will always be slightly golden in color. But keep in mind that this type of "white" flour will also give you more nutritious bread with a more intense flavor; especially when working with sourdoughs, starters, or long fermentation.

Unfortunately, high-extraction stone-ground flour is difficult for North American home bakers to find, but do not let this concern you. For the recipes in this book, you may substitute our sifted ("white") stone-ground spelt and wheat flours with North American white (roller mill) spelt or wheat flours with 12.5 percent protein. The same goes for pastry flour of 9 to 10 percent protein.

Should you want to aim for that lovely golden color in your usually white bread, we suggest trying the following: Make a mix of 85 percent white flour with 15 percent stone-ground whole-grain flour (the whole-grain flour should be finely ground; if not, take out the coarser bran particles using a fine-meshed sieve). This is not truly white flour that's comparable to ours, but it is a fair approximation and the best available to the home bakers for whom this book is intended.

Finally, it is always a good idea to carefully observe the water absorption levels of your dough—this cannot be stressed enough. For this reason the stated amounts of liquids in the recipes are always approximate, because we know that, depending on the type of flour you use (stone milled or roller milled, or both), and the humidity level (high or low), the dough will need slightly more or less water on different days.

You will learn exactly how to make such precise adjustments; experience will give you that "sense for the dough" that will help you make wonderful Nordic bread with the ingredients you have at hand, especially if you believe, as we do, that successful bread baking relies on sound methods and attention to detail. We weigh everything—from salt and fresh yeast to flour and water. Wonderful bread can only ever be properly reproduced if you know exactly what you've put into your dough, and in what quantity. Cups and measuring jugs are great for pouring liquids; however, they will never provide you with the kind of precision necessary to transform baking into a continuously joyous experience. So buy yourself a scale, pull out the dough scraper, and you're ready to go *Home Baked*!

Happy baking, and enjoy!

Hanne Risgaard

Preface

At the start of every August, I keep an eye on the weather. Is high pressure coming? Will the nights be dry and mild, the skies cloudless and clear? If the outlook is good for the nights around the twelfth of August, I fetch the sunbed and some coffee and find a good spot in the middle of the lawn. With the noises of the night chiming out against the silence, and the dew sending the coffee fragrance bursting into life, I take my seat at one of nature's great performances, the "Tears of St. Lawrence"—the hundreds of shooting stars caused by Earth's annual, breathtaking meeting with the Perseid meteor shower.

I'm also a regular at another of nature's extravaganzas. The scene is set in the deep, reed-bed forests close to the German border. Here, I am definitely not alone as the audience comes pouring in. This show is a blockbuster, and the question is, how many will fit on stage tonight? We are waiting for the spectacle known as the "Black Sun." As twilight shifts toward the nighttime, thousands of starlings begin to gather. They flock above the forests, filling the sky, back and forth, near and far, high up in the air and then right back down to the ground: a swaying dance of curious designs, shifting shapes, and unpredictable waves.

Some people have seen pictures of the starlings' ballet, but only those who have stood at the edges of the reed forest have experienced the deafening statements in these mysterious, swirling glyphs. They are vast! And the noise is, too. It won't calm down until darkness finally falls and the starlings settle into the reeds, surrounded by thousands of fellow players.

I set out deliberately to see the Tears of St. Lawrence and the Black Sun, wind and weather allowing. But there are other experiences in nature that we cannot plan to watch. If we ever happen to see them, it is an unexpected gift.

A summer morning. Early, and already mild. Soft, low light over the field. Green ears of rye, delicately touched with violet. Windless calm . . . a weak breeze . . . and suddenly, it's there—or is it? A transparent cloud of pollen lifts up over the field, released by the rye, like dust on the wings of pixies, stirred by the dance of the fairies. Slowly, slowly it moves, almost invisible. The softest gust, and then a bittersweet smell of grain reaches the nose. An overwhelming sensation. A magic moment, making its promises to the coming harvest.

Making bread strikes a mysteriously
prehistoric cord somewhere inside us.
Alongside the mental satisfaction,
you discover new different gastronomic pleasures,
that enriches you, and those around you.
Lionel Poilâne, master baker, Paris

INTRODUCTION

There is magic in grain: when it's in the field, when the grains are ground to flour in the mill, when the flour is turned to dough, and when the dough is baked to bread. The magic is present all along, even if what happens on the journey from grain to crumb is explained by science. Because on any given day, there are always those extra little factors, sparked by a particular moment in time: the wind and the weather, your mood, and the yeast or the sourdough in the flour. It's these unique extra elements that mean you can never be quite sure of how your efforts will be rewarded when you set out to transform the simplest of the simple—flour, water, yeast, and salt—into a crisp, tasty, aromatic bread.

My fascination with this particular mix of knowledge, craft, and that little spark of magic is the reason I have written this book. As such, it has two intentions: One is to present the virtues of grains and flour, which, at their best, are fantastic products, direct from nature, and should be valued and treated with respect. In a world fighting lifestyle diseases such as obesity, diabetes, cardiac disease, and cancer, scientists have long recommended good grain produce as one of the means to reduce the risk of these threats. But the sad fact is that 94 percent of all Danes (and a figure just as staggering in the United States) do not eat enough good, wholesome bread and are therefore not getting enough dietary fiber, vitamins, and minerals; a modern health dilemma, very easily remedied simply by eating a lot more whole-grain products—and this, as luck would have it, is easily attainable without compromising flavor.

The book's other message is that it is simple, rewarding, and fun to bake. Even if some recipes might deal with apparently "expert" terms such as *biga*, *pâte fermentée*, *poolish*, *sourdough*, and *long-time fermentation*, my message is that you shouldn't let yourself be limited by what you feel you don't know. Baking is a craft, which everybody can learn, but it's at its best when driven by passion, expectation, and joy! It might be that in the beginning you need to be a bit more disciplined, following the recipes word for word, until you begin to get that special knowledge in your fingertips for the dough, and an eye and an ear for when a loaf is fully baked. But from there on in, once you've picked up the techniques, you can free yourself from the recipes and begin to experiment. It's just like riding a bike: Once you've learned how, you'll know it for the rest of your life.

The Story of Skærtoft Mølle

CAN AN ADVENTURE BEGIN WITH A QUESTION?

Late summer, visiting a park in London. Warm sun and a lunchtime atmosphere. I was sitting on a bench with my eyes closed, enjoying the heat. Suddenly, somebody asks, *"What fingerprint will you leave on the world?"* It's an old man, who has sat down next to me and who clearly wants to talk. And so we do, but without my ever answering his provocative question. The gauntlet, however, had been thrown.

"What fingerprint will you leave on the world?" The question would not let go of me and demanded an answer. And that answer appeared, on August 15, 2003, a landmark date in our family history. That day my husband Jørgen and I were sitting in our separate cars, heading for our respective meetings, and listening to the same show on the radio. At ten past nine the host, a professional cook named Nanna Simonsen, welcomed two experts who had been invited to speak that day: pastry chef Thorleif Kristensen, owner of the Music Patisserie, Copenhagen; and the academic Ane Bodil Søgaard, who has conducted research into grain at the Carlsberg brewery and at the Royal Veterinary and Agricultural University.

The day's culinary discussion is all about flour!

Most of the broadcast's two hours was spent on the incredibly bad flour and terrible bread that the Danes seem happy to settle for. Part of the problem is that flour and bread are among the oldest processed foodstuffs and are thought of as so common, everyday, and unsexy that they can end up being treated with indifference. The result is that neither flour nor bread end up carrying the same expectations of flavor and nutrition that are otherwise demanded from our other foods.

Flour producers, bakers, and the bread industry were all getting a real hammering from the guests on the show. Fortunately, though, the guests were able to offer alternative solutions. Bodil Søgaard outlined, with broad brushstrokes, the formula of how to make the best flour in the world, and both guests and the host wound up completely united in the idea that if only proper flour was made freely available a bread revolution could be created in Denmark.

That broadcast really hit home.

For some time prior to that, Jørgen and I, along with our daughter Marie-Louise, had discussed any possibilities our farm might offer us to leave a decent fingerprint on the world. Because we were farming grain, the idea of making flour had been put on the table . . . but Jørgen had hesitated. As the fourth generation at Skærtoft, he felt it made good sense to be a part-time farmer . . . but a miller?

When we came home that August evening, however, there was no longer any doubt: We should give flour a go. We would try—and this was said modestly, of course!—to make the World's Best Flour . . . or get as close as possible. It would be organic, stone-ground flour, with the germ and bran left in. Pure, no additives, milled only to order, and with a naturally short shelf-life. Flavor and nutritional value would not be mutually exclusive but would go naturally hand in hand.

Once the decision was made, things happened very quickly. In the beginning we worked alone, with the skills we had. When problems appeared that we couldn't solve ourselves, and there were many, we looked for help, from the best we could find. And so it was that on June 1, 2004, after ten months of hard work—from us and from many other people—the very first bags of stone-ground flour made their way from Skærtoft Mølle (mill).

There was no time to celebrate with champagne, because we had to make flour the day after that, the day after that, and then the next day after that! At that time none of us could imagine the journey we had in store for us. Fortunately, though, there has always been time for morning coffee, shared with home-baked bread.

*"The real voyage of discovery lies
not in seeking new landscapes,
but in having new eyes."*

Marcel Proust

FROM VISION TO REALITY

Organic farming is really very simple: It's about working with nature, not against it. The farmer does this partly by cycling different crops throughout the fields—what is known as *crop rotation*—to prevent the soil from becoming depleted of nutrients. Everyone who has a vegetable patch knows that the crops do well when moved around, and this is exactly what the farmer does, just on a different scale. In our fields at Skærtoft, the crops in the rotation are not vegetables, but wheat, spelt/barley, rye/oats, and clover. Clover is included in the rotation at Skærtoft because, again, we set out to work with nature, in this case by using the clover's fantastic ability to supply the soil with nitrogen through its roots. Without nitrogen, plants will starve, and on an organic farm, it can't be supplied by means of artificial fertilizer. It must find its way into the soil by some other method—and that's where the clover comes in.

In addition to these factors, there is also the crucial choice of grain varieties to consider, which must be robust enough to cope with and even prevent pests and diseases. Organic farmers do not use toxins to get rid of pests, so the grain must be able to stand on its own.

Finally, it is also important to make sure that between the crop fields there are untouched borders, strips of land that remain as either hedgerow or permanent grassland. Here, many beneficial species of insects—the ones we see as "helpers"—can thrive, feeding on unwanted pests. Again: This is working with nature, being on its side, and allowing the innate intelligence of its systems to support us.

The deeper we immerse ourselves in finding out the qualities and capabilities of the different grains, the more fascinated we become by the diversity to which we have access. There are parallels between us and wine farmers, for example. They must know about the soil, the location of the fields, the different flavors and varieties of grapes, the terroir, the different harvest methods . . . ultimately, the entire process that turns grapes into wine. It's exactly the same with us, but with grain instead of grapes and flour instead of wine.

Of course, as with the wine farmer, there is also that unpredictable factor to consider: the weather throughout the growing season. This will have a decisive influence on the quality of the year's harvest, no matter how good the farmer is at his trade. That's how it is, and we wouldn't have it any other way.

When the Harvest Is In

Harvest season is also a time of lab tests, which are carried out on the different batches of grain from our fields, just as grains sourced from other suppliers will also be tested. The tests regarding falling number as well as protein and gluten are of particular interest. The falling number tells us whether the grain can bake at all. Protein and gluten content tell us if the grain can be milled for protein-rich bread flour or for cake flour, which has a low protein content, or whether it should be sold for animal feed.

An important part of the lab tests is also to guarantee that the crops are free from the hazardous mycotoxins that are produced by a group of *Aspergillus* (mold) species.

Myth

Toxins in grains are unwelcome guests, which fortunately appear only extremely rarely. When they are discovered, the food authorities react instantly, with all products under suspicion being recalled and destroyed.

I have been told a few times—always as a fact that isn't up for "discussion"—that organic grain, and therefore organic flour, is particularly susceptible to being poisoned with toxins. Well, fortunately, the truth is that these two things *do not* go together. Toxins have nothing to do with organic farming and everything to do with bad farming practice. The risk of toxins occurs when the grain is not stored correctly. If the grains have the correct water content, and the storage facilities are dry and hygienic, any risk of toxins' occurring is extremely small. But we always test anyway, to be on the safe side!

Grading

In the coffee world there is a term known as "grading." It refers to the very thorough sorting process that coffee beans are put through to ensure that only the perfect beans—in terms of size, shape, and color—earn the "best quality" label. Because we wish to make our flour to as high a standard as possible, we have sneaked a peek at this coffee bean process.

If you grade your bread grains as part of the cleaning process—which all grains go through—then only the perfect grains make the grade. This results in a "just right" balance between endosperm, bran, and germ and is the reason we grade all our grains this way. It results in a lot of leftovers . . . but the grains that aren't used for flour are never really wasted. Anything that cannot be used in the mill gets used as feed for cows and pigs and for birds and other wildlife in the winter.

Stone Mill versus Roller Mill

Most of the flour sold in Denmark, as in the USA, is produced on steel rollers, as it is the cheapest and most efficient method. The steel roller makes it easy to separate the flour into bran, germ, and endosperm. By a large margin most of the flour on the market that is made using this process fails to contain the healthy germ.

An alternative to the roller mill is the stone mill, an ancient technology by which the grains are crushed between two large stone discs. The discs have patterns etched into the grinding surfaces, to improve the grinding effect on the grains. On a stone mill the component parts of the grain are not separated as efficiently as they are on a roller mill. Hence, stone-milled flour will always contain some of the germ and the bran. Correspondingly, it will also contain higher quantities of a long list of nutrients.

At Skærtoft we make flour on stone mills. By setting the discs precisely, we ensure that all of the component parts of the grain are present in both whole-grain and white flour. Naturally, the bran content, and therefore the amount of fiber, is less in the white flour; however, the vitamins and minerals from the germ, along with those parts of the bran that are fine enough to pass through the 200 μm (micron) sieves, are preserved. So as I've said, our white flour isn't white, but slightly golden. The gold-brown color is retained in the finished bread, which is both healthier and tastier than bread made from very white flours consisting only of endosperm.

TO BAKE BREAD

The Oven

It pays to invest in a good oven. However, regardless of quality, every oven will have its own "personality." You simply must get to know your oven to get the best out of it. Good advice is to check its temperature with an oven thermometer. Even in new ovens, there may be differences between its stated temperature settings and its *actual* inside temperature.

Also, you should check whether the oven bakes evenly throughout all the oven space or if it's necessary to turn the sheet pan 180° halfway through.

If you use a convection oven, the temperature is usually set 50 to 70°F lower than a regular oven. And do remember that every time you open the oven door, the temperature inside the oven will drop by around 70°F, so try to open it as little as possible.

Finally, it's a good idea to "bake with your eyes and ears." Use your experience to determine when the crust has turned the appropriate color and if it sounds right when you tap your knuckle on the underside of the loaf. If these methods aren't conclusive, then use a probe thermometer. Push the thermometer into the very heart of the loaf; when this core temperature reaches 208°F, the bread is finished.

Kitchen Machinery

I am in no way a kitchen Luddite, and I fully acknowledge that I love my food processor, my blender, my juicer, my mandolin, my ice machine, and everything else that I've bought for my kitchen. The best thing I own is "Teddy," my mixer, who bails me out when I don't have time to enjoy working the dough by hand, or when the recipe demands more muscle power than I can manage.

THE ESSENTIAL EQUIPMENT

When previous generations baked, the tools they needed were simply a bowl, a table, and an oven. It's the same basic equipment that's needed today, too, but of course it's both practical and fun to have a little more to play with.

Boiled down to a minimum, here's what I use:
- Work table
- Bowl
- Scales
- Plastic scraper
- Plastic bag
- Dish towel
- Parchment paper
- Oven

Any other equipment I have in my kitchen just makes baking easier, more creative, and more fun.

Work Surfaces

When situated in the same room, work surfaces of wood, stone, and steel all have the same temperature, but wood has an insulating effect that works well with bread doughs. Marble, stone, or steel surfaces have no insulating effect and are therefore suitable for all fatty doughs because they keep the doughs cool.

Metal Dough Cutter

A metal dough cutter is good for dividing the dough with clean cuts and is also efficient for cleaning your table once you have finished.

Thermometer

A digital baking thermometer shows you when your bread is done, how warm your dough ingredients are, and whether the temperature in your oven is really what it says on the display. As I mentioned earlier, you will be amazed how often the two things don't match up. When starting up a sourdough, I can't do without a thermometer.

Water Spray Bottle

By misting water from a spray bottle into the oven immediately before and after putting in the dough, you fill the oven space with steam, which settles on the top side of the dough, thereby keeping it moist and elastic, and ensuring that it rises in the best possible way. The steam also means that the finished bread has a more golden color and the crust a more intense flavor.

Spray bottles can be bought in kitchen supply stores, garden centers, and hardware stores.

Mixing Bowl

A plastic bowl or a pottery bowl works just fine. I prefer working with a stainless metal bowl, without rubber grips on the base. These bowls are light, can easily be turned on the table, and don't break if I drop them.

Couche, or Baker's Linen

When you proof baguettes, for instance, it's nice to work with a linen couche, or baker's linen. Dust the linen with flour, place the baguettes onto it, and pull up folds between them. The folds should be high enough to prevent the baguettes from sticking together as they rise.

The couche should be brushed/shaken thoroughly after use but never washed. Once you have used the couche a few times, the flour will have settled into the surface, giving it a non-stick effect.

Measuring Cups and Jugs

Of course I have measuring cups and jugs in my kitchen. Not for measuring out liquids— they are much too imprecise for that—but as convenient containers to pour from.

Proofing Basket

Proofing baskets (bannetons) exist in several shapes, with and without a lining, and are used for proofing doughs that are so soft that proofing them in a freestanding fashion isn't possible. You can also use the proofing basket just to create decorative effects: The coiled ones in particular make beautiful patterns on the dough. Before proofing baskets are used, they should be dusted on the inside with flour, to prevent the dough from sticking to the sides and bottom.

The baskets are cleaned with a stiff brush, or a vacuum cleaner (used only for this purpose) if required. They must not be washed with water or put into the oven. The more you use the baskets, the less they need to be dusted with flour. As with the couches, the flour creates a coating, so that the basket almost has a nonstick effect on the inside.

Dough Scraper

A plastic scraper is indispensable! I use one when I mix, work, divide, fold, and shape my doughs, as well as when I am cleaning my hands, bowl, and work surface.

Kitchen Timer

When the kitchen is running at full tilt, and that is quite often, it is nice to be able to set a timer so I don't forget the next stage of whatever it is I'm working on. It's not the most important thing on my equipment list, but it does give me a nice, secure feeling and limits any silly mistakes, such as proofing bread for too long.

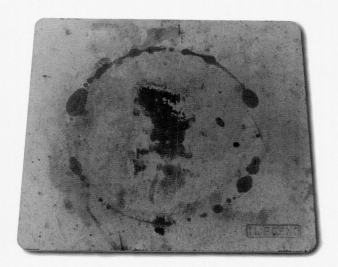

Baking Stone

You can buy an unglazed tile in a hardware store, put it on a wire rack on the bottom shelf of the oven, and you have your baking stone. You can also buy a pizza stone, which you can get in kitchen supply stores. Both stones, once they are heated through, approximate the effect of an old-fashioned stone oven. When the dough is eased directly onto the hot stone, it is quickly and evenly penetrated by the heat. The crumb becomes moister, the crust more crisp, the flavor more pronounced. The bread will also stay fresh longer. If you don't have a baking stone, you can use a sheet pan, putting the bread directly onto that—but only when working with high temperatures. As with the stone the very hot sheet pan will prevent the dough from sticking fast.

Knife

A super-sharp knife, a scalpel or a razor blade set on a small, thin, flat metal stick—what French bakers call a "lame"—is indispensable for scoring (*not* ripping) the dough, before it goes into the oven. By scoring the dough you control the way the dough bursts when it is baked. You can also use the way the dough is scored as decoration, or as a personal signature on the bread.

Resting Tent

A large freezer bag, of at least ten gallons, makes an ideal "resting tent." Put the bowl in the bag when leaving the dough to rest, and close it with a chip clip. That way you keep the dough's moisture in the bag, stopping the surface of the dough from drying out and at the same time ensuring a draft-free environment.

Peel

The type of peel that most people will recognize is the pizza peel, which is used when loading a pizza into a scorching hot oven. The long handle means that you can keep a safe distance from the hot stone. Peels come in different shapes and sizes, to fit the bread you wish to bake. Slim and long for baguettes; shorter and wider for freestanding loaves.

Before you set your proofed dough onto the peel, you must sprinkle the peel lightly with what I like to call "rolling stones," types of coarse meal such as cornmeal or semolina. This will prevent the dough from sticking to the peel when being eased onto the baking stone or sheet pan.

Scales

Good scales are invaluable. They must be able to weigh precisely down to the gram, and they must have a tare function.

THE BASIC INGREDIENTS

Every time I mix the ingredients (flour, yeast, salt, and water) and two or three hours later hold up a golden, aromatic loaf, with a crispy crust and a soft and savory crumb, I feel a little high. It is pure magic that with these few, totally different ingredients, I can make one of the most fundamental sources of nutrition that we have: bread.

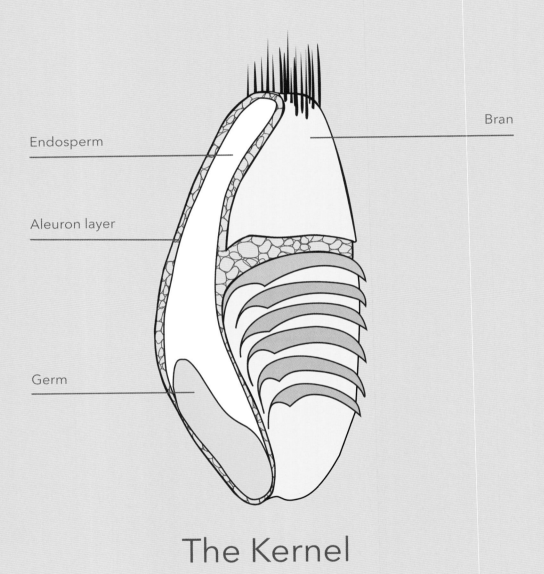

Endosperm

Aleuron layer

Germ

Bran

The Kernel

A kernel of wheat, like the one pictured above, is no bigger than 0.1 to 0.2 inches long, but it is a little powerhouse, bursting with the energy created by nature over thousands of growing seasons.

FLOUR

The Bran

The outer layer of the kernel is called the bran. In nature the job of the bran is to protect the endosperm and the germ. As long as the bran is whole and intact, the grain is able to germinate and can remain so for many hundreds of years. In terms of weight the bran accounts for approximately 15 percent of the kernel.

Dietary Fibers
Bran is the primary source of dietary fiber in flour, and grain products in general are our most important source of dietary fiber. It is recommended that we consume around 3 ounces of dietary fiber a day and that two-thirds of this should come from grain products, preferably from whole-grain bread. In truth, only a small minority of people actually manage this, which is unfortunate. Modern research has definite proof that dietary fibers, containing antioxidants, can prevent cancer.

Dietary fibers are split up into two categories: soluble and insoluble.

The soluble fibers help to regulate blood sugar levels, reduce cholesterol, and enhance the body's ability to take up the nutrients in our diet. The insoluble fibers ensure good digestion, preventing constipation.

Incidentally, the bran content of the flour is not dependent on the size of the bran particles—fiber is fiber! When there is bran in the flour, you have dietary fiber, whether the particles are large or small. In effect this means that coarse whole-grain flour doesn't necessarily have a higher dietary fiber content than fine whole-grain flour. Conventional white flour consisting only of endosperm has no fiber content, whereas the white flour we make with the stone mill at Skærtoft has a 5 percent dietary fiber content. When we produce white flour, we take out only the coarsest pieces of bran, leaving the finer bran particles to add nutrition and flavor to the flour. But this means, of course, that we do not produce totally white-colored flour—we go for the golden!

The Germ

The germ of a kernel can be compared to the yolk of an egg. It is where the new life begins, so it is filled with everything that's needed to ensure the new plant a good start in life: vitamins D and E, folic acid, phytic acid, and fatty acids, to mention some of the most important. Vitamin E and folic acid in particular are interesting; we know that vitamin E, which is an antioxidant, enhances fertility, and that folic acid is important for a pregnant mother and her developing child.

The germ makes up no more than 3 to 5 percent of the total weight of the kernel. It is contained in a neat little package, meaning it can be easily separated by modern industry's roller mill method, which is primarily interested in retaining the endosperm. The superhealthy germ is regarded as an unwanted presence, because the oils contained in it increase the risk of rancidity. Or to put it another way, the germ reduces the shelf life of the flour.

Long Shelf Life
If there's anything that retailers and the flour industry are united on here, it is the desire to give flour a very long shelf life. To capitalize on that desire, millers take the oily germ out of the flour, and the risk of rancidity with it. In health terms this is a catastrophe! Scientific evidence has long demonstrated that flour without the germ loses both flavor and nutritional value. Evidence has also shown that the fresher the flour, the greater value it has both nutritionally and gastronomically. Yet it is still common practice to remove the germ from both white flour and certain types of whole-grain flour. So the consumer is consistently sold a product of far lesser worth than that which nature has to offer. This situation could be quickly changed, however, if retailers and industry were to shift their priorities from long shelf life to health and flavor.

The Endosperm

The endosperm is the grain's well-protected "lunch box," which only gets consumed the minute the grain starts germinating and creating a brand-new plant with roots, stalk, leaves, and ears. The endosperm makes up about 80 percent of the total weight of the grain and consists primarily of starch and protein.

Starch affects the structure and flavor of the finished loaf. The content of the protein known as gluten determines whether a harvest can be used for bread flour or pastry flour or—and this applies to most of the wheat grown in Denmark—whether it would best end up as animal feed.

Gluten
The gluten proteins make up between 8 and 18 percent of the endosperm in a wheat grain. The consistency of gluten is almost like chewing gum. If you take a handful of "whole" wheat grains in your mouth and chew them thoroughly, after a while you will be able to blow bubbles from the resulting substance.

Wheat flour's ability to be baked depends on both the quality and quantity of the gluten. The quality depends on the chosen wheat variety and is therefore genetically determined; whereas the quantity of gluten in a wheat harvest is influenced, among other factors, by the weather during the growing season. The more sun, the more gluten!

Gluten consists of large molecules. When the flour is poured into the bowl, these molecules bristle in all directions. One of dough-making's functions is to form the molecules into a configuration of continuous strings. The gluten network, necessary to create elasticity and strength in the finished dough, is thereby formed. When the yeast cells begin to work, breaking down the dough's carbohydrates into alcohol and carbon dioxide, it is the strength and elasticity of this network that determines the extent to which the dough can expand before the network will rupture; in other words, how well the dough will rise. The gases trapped in the dough give the finished loaf its porous structure.

Some people cannot tolerate gluten and therefore can't eat food containing, for example, wheat, spelt, rye, barley, or oats. However, there is a huge difference between a full gluten allergy (known as celiac disease) and having an intolerance toward wheat. Many people who cannot eat wheat thrive perfectly well on spelt, even though spelt is also a wheat variety.

YEAST

Yeast, which is what makes dough rise, consists of a unicellular microorganism from the vast fungus family. Both organic and nonorganic yeast are based on a yeast strain with the Latin name *Saccharomyces cerevisiae*. It is as fussy as its name is long, demanding particular conditions in which to work: nutrients, water, warmth, and oxygen. But when these four demands are met, it delivers in abundance—something you can clearly see when looking at well-risen dough.

Before the yeast becomes active in the dough, enzymes in the flour must break down the endosperm's starch to sugar, which the yeast then turns into carbon dioxide and alcohol. The carbon dioxide is what makes the dough rise. Some of the alcohol evaporates when the bread is baked, but what's left of it adds to the flavor. The amount of yeast in a recipe will determine the resting time, the flavor, and the length of time the bread will stay fresh. A general rule is that small amounts of yeast and long resting periods provide the best flavor and the longest-keeping bread. If you use large amounts of yeast, especially nonorganic, then its flavor will dominate and your bread will become stale and bland in a matter of hours.

Organic yeast performs a little more slowly than nonorganic yeast. However, your reward for this extra fermenting time is fantastic-tasting bread.

	Manufacture of organic yeast	Manufacture of conventional yeast
Sugar source	Organic grain	Molasses
Nitrogen source	Organic grain	Ammonia (NH_3), ammonium salts
pH regulator	No pH level regulation necessary	Acids (e.g., sulfuric acid), alkalis (e.g., caustic soda)
Processing and growth substances	Sufficiently present in natural media	Synthetic vitamins and mineral salts
Antifoaming agent	Organic sunflower oil	Synthetic antifoaming agent
Rinsing	Unnecessary	Two times
Wastewater	Raw material for other products	Disposal difficult

A "Myth" about Nonorganic versus Organic Yeast

Throughout the years I have spoken to many people, including professional bakers, who refuse to believe that organic yeast even exists. Naturally, this isn't true. The explanation for such stubbornness lies not with ignorance but somewhere in Brussels in the past. In 1992 the EU decided to define what constitutes an organic product. Yeast, along with salt, was filed under "produce not connected to agriculture." Thus the opportunity to market yeast as organic was lost. But unlike salt, yeast is clearly tied to agriculture because of the raw materials in which the yeast cells are grown. And it is the difference between these raw materials that determines whether yeast is organic or not.

Nonorganic yeast is grown primarily on sugar molasses. This is sourced from conventional agriculture, which routinely utilizes artificial fertilizers and pesticides. At the industrial stage of nonorganic yeast production, several substances are added, such as ammonia, ammonium salts, sulfuric acid, synthetic vitamins, and inorganic salts, along with a synthetic antifoaming agent. The wastewater from this line of production is classified as difficult to biodegrade because of its pollution risk. As shown here in the table, organic yeast production only uses organic raw materials, which means that the resulting wastewater can have other direct uses, such as in the production of organic sourdough for bakeries.

The EU prohibition of naming organic yeast "organic" has called for many creative solutions. In Austria yeast from the German organic company Agrano has been marketed as "organic cereal produce with yeast." Officially correct, yes, but not very elegant—and definitely not consumer friendly.

Fortunately, in 2008 the list of organic produce was adjusted and updated by the EU, so beginning January 1, 2009, it became legal to market organic yeast as exactly what it is: organic yeast!

SALT

Salt (sodium chloride) plays an important role when you bake bread.
- It influences the flavor.
- It strengthens the gluten.
- It prolongs the life of the bread.
- It gives color to the crust.

It is often argued that reducing or totally excluding salt can decrease the risk of heart disease, among other things. But salt is not dangerous to healthy people; on the contrary, if we get too little salt, it affects both our body's water content and our ability to get rid of toxins.

I think that, with a little common sense, it should be no problem at all to use salt in a normal, everyday context. On the other hand, it is a very good idea to avoid all the oversalted industrial products we can buy today in any supermarket, gas station, or convenience store, such as chips, soups, instant meals, and so on. If you avoid these, you will reduce your salt intake, thereby making room for a sensible, everyday use of salt—a very important factor when it comes to flavor.

When you bake bread, salt enhances the bread's flavor and the color of the crust—but only when used in proper amounts. A good rule is that it should represent 2 percent of the total weight of the flour. For example, if you make dough with 500 grams of flour, you should use 10 grams of salt. If you will be adding whole or cracked grains, you must add their weight to the flour weight and measure the amount of salt accordingly. I recommend weighing all ingredients, and that includes salt. Measuring spoons are imprecise—and just think of the difference in weight between one teaspoon of fine table salt and one teaspoon of coarse cooking salt.

Salt does more than add flavor to bread; it also acts as a regulator for enzyme activity, for instance in sourdoughs. Therefore, it is important that you follow instructions carefully, saltwise, when you make starters or sourdoughs. If salt and yeast come into direct contact with each other, the salt will lessen the effect of the yeast, because of salt's water-attracting properties. So it is important to keep salt and yeast separate, until it's time to mix them up with the flour.

Salt exists in many varieties, and with almost as many flavors. From fine salt, coarse salt, "sydesalt" from Læsø, and "Fleur de Sel" from Camargue to the crisp, white flakes of Maldon Salt or the slightly moist sea salt known as "grey salt." My own favorite comes from Ile de Ré, by the French Atlantic coast. It tastes fantastic but is unfortunately not too easy to obtain.

WATER

An increasing number of baking books recommend the use of distilled water, in particular when starting up a sourdough. The argument is that wild yeast, which is a prerequisite for starting a sourdough, is very sensitive toward even tiny amounts of chemicals. If your regular water supply has any chemical residue in it, it might ruin your chances for making a robust sourdough. My advice is this: Use regular water from the faucet whenever possible, as long as your supply is safe and reliable. Better yet, try home-filtered water, an inexpensive, easy, and effective solution. Should your sourdough fail, *then* try distilled water . . . but remember that from an organic and environmental point of view distilled water is not always the best idea.

And then there's the issue of water temperature. How lukewarm is "lukewarm" when a recipe states "lukewarm water"? Is the instruction "an appropriate temperature" any more helpful? Experience will furnish you with the ability to judge when the water temperature in a recipe is just right for kick-starting fermentation. But if you want to be 100 percent sure, you can use a very simple equation to provide you with an exact answer. All you need is a thermometer and to know what temperature you'd like the finished dough to be. The equation looks like this:

Desired dough temperature multiplied by 2, minus current flour temperature, equals required water temperature.

Let's say you'd like a dough temperature of 82°F and the flour temperature is 68°F. The equation would look like this:

82 x 2 = 164
164 – 68 = 96°F

If you store your flour in a cool place—for example at 57°F—you'll get the following result:

82 x 2 = 164
164 – 57 = 107°F

For all home bakers mixing by hand, it is as simple as that!

EXTRA INGREDIENTS

Start out with the four basic ingredients—flour, water, salt, and yeast—then start adding or substituting some of the ingredients in the recipes . . . and soon you're well into what I call "variations on the theme of bread baking"! There are so many possibilities, ones you find in recipes and ones you find out yourself through experimentation.

Here is some inspiration:

Special Flours

Sifted rye flour: for rye bread and rye crackers and for adding flavor to wheat bread.

Sifted barley flour: ideal for adding flavor to both wheat bread and coarser types of bread; very suitable for crackers or crispbread and excellent for ordinary pancakes and Russian pancakes (blini).

Pastry flour: flour with 9 to 10 percent protein made from wheat. It is the protein content that determines what the flour should be used for; for example, low-protein pastry flour versus high-protein bread flour. Pastry flour should be used when no yeast is required; for instance, in pies, tarts, and cookies.

Durum flour: the hard wheat flour you cannot do without when making wonderful Italian bread classics.

Malt flour: malted wheat or barley grain that has then been milled to flour. I prefer nondiastatic malt flour, which has no enzyme activity. Used sparingly, it brings a beautiful color as well as an intensified flavor to the bread.

Rolled oats or barley flakes: They add flavor and texture to bread and are really good in cookies.

Liquids

Milk (no skimmed varieties), buttermilk, and sour milk products (e.g., plain yogurt), are lovely in bread and give you softer and whiter bread. Milk products add protein to the finished bread. Beer, hard cider, and apple juice each contribute their own special flavor and are very suitable for bread. And dark malt beer is pretty much indispensable in rye bread.

Eggs

In baking, eggs contribute protein along with calcium, iron, potassium, and, of course, the fluid contained in the egg. Coagulation of the egg happens during baking and provides you with a soft and uniform crumb. The yolk adds both color and flavor to the crust.

Oils and Fats

Butter, fat, and vegetable oils make the crumb softer and improve, to some extent, the longevity of the bread. Flavorful oils, such as olive oil, naturally contribute their own aromatic quality.

Sugar and Other Sweeteners

Sugar, honey (liquid or set), and syrup all add natural sweetness to the bread and give the crust a golden color.

Seeds and Grains

There are many possibilities, and your own tastes will guide you in which ones to use. General rules are that if the seeds and grains have a delicate flavor, you may use a lot of them; for example, sunflower seeds, pumpkin seeds, linseed and poppy seeds. If the flavor is more intense, however—say, fennel and caraway seeds—you should regard them as spices and use accordingly.

Nuts

I love nuts, especially hazelnuts. Toast them lightly in a dry frying pan at medium temperature until the skin has darkened in color. Rub the skin off using a dish towel, thereby turning the nuts a light color, then try. Wonderful!

Walnuts are my other favorite. In addition to adding a wonderful flavor, they turn the bread the most beautiful brown color, with a dash of purple.

Dried Fruit

Apricots, raisins, dates, cranberries, blueberries: There are so many possibilities. The fruits all contribute to texture and flavor. As with seeds and grains, they should be used in moderation. Unless, of course, you want to bake an actual "fruit bread" and not a "bread with fruit"!

BREAD BAKING
STEP BY STEP

It would of course be perfectly possible to grow grain and make flour without also baking bread . . . but taking that final step undeniably adds to the fun and makes things more challenging, turning the expression "from farm to plate" into more than just a saying. So with our lives already filled with books about grain, flour, and baking, we continued to gather important and practical inspiration from Denmark, Sweden, England, and Germany from—among others—Aurion, Saltå Kværn, Shipton Mill, Sharpham Park, and Bohlsener Mühle; and we never missed out on any occasion to visit inspiring Master Bakers like Richard Bertinet at The Bertinet Kitchen and Andrew Whitley at Bread Matters Ltd. Again and again Marie-Louise and I participated in bread classes and workshops, until, after years as nomadic baking novices, we started our own bread classes in Skærtoft Stable Kitchen, based on the motto that "what you have learned, you should pass on to others."

At the heart of what we have learned from Richard Bertinet is his traditional French way of working the dough, which has completely changed the way we make bread. The technique is perfectly suitable for stone-ground flours with the germ and the bran preserved in them, like the flours we make at Skærtoft. With too much flour and too little liquid in the dough, stone-ground flour can easily deliver bread that is too heavy. The French principles, however, allow it to flourish in all kinds of bread, from the more substantial farmers' breads to Italian ciabattas full of air and crusty French baguettes to tougher American bagels. And naturally, all other wonderful types of bread.

10 Good Bits of Advice
Good advice, such as that listed below, should not be followed blindly. It is better to evaluate your own experiences against others', observing and understanding in the process what is actually going on when you bake. In this way you will gain control over the whole process, and once you have achieved this, you can free yourself from "prescribed" advice and "constraining" recipes.

Luck follows the well prepared.

Jane Aamund

1: gathering and weighing

Gather all your ingredients before starting, and weigh them. Forget measuring cups or jugs: They are imprecise. Instead, use good digital scales with a tare function. It is a good idea to let all your ingredients warm to room temperature before you start making your dough, unless otherwise stated in the recipe!

2: mixing

Mix all dry ingredients. If you are using fresh yeast, rub it into the flour before adding the salt. Then add the fluid, and mix thoroughly with your plastic scraper until there are no dry bits left in the bowl.

Because I work with somewhat wet dough, it is not usually necessary to dissolve the yeast in liquid before mixing it with the flour. When rubbed in thoroughly, the yeast will dissolve just fine in moist dough. *Important*: You should never add more flour to the dough than is specified in the recipe. You can, however, adjust the wetness of the dough with fluid. Flour absorbs more or less liquid depending on the humidity and temperature of your kitchen, for example. Once mixed, the dough should have a sticky, porridgelike texture.

Until you have figured out the routine, it may be difficult for you to sense when the dough is appropriately moist. In the majority of my recipes, fluid is equivalent to 70 percent of the total quantity of flour. Thus, 1,000 grams of flour takes 700 grams of water. Sometimes though, as mentioned, you will have to add more or less liquid to the dough to obtain the best result. Here you should always remind yourself that "wetter is better."

3: working the dough

Once the dough has been thoroughly mixed, scrape it from the bowl onto a clean, dry work surface. This will create a top side to the dough, which you should try to keep through to the finished loaf. Start by making your hands into mitten shapes, and then sliding them beneath the dough—one from either side—while letting your thumbs rest lightly on the top side. Stretch the dough to either side in soft but firm movements, almost like tickling the dough on its belly. We say that we "air" the dough. After stretching it ten to fifteen times, you will notice that the top side changes and that the uneven porridgelike dough becomes increasingly smooth and shiny. When you have tried "airing" it like this a couple of times, you will feel more confident about handling the soft dough. Use your scraper to gather the dough.

And now it's time to work the dough "the Bertinet way":
Let your fingers slide beneath the dough, supporting the top side with your thumbs, and lift the dough at its far end so that the top side is facing you. Swing the lower part of the dough away from you and slap it down onto the table. Stretch the dough toward you, then fold the dough in half, by folding the part you are holding across the dough that is now stuck to the table. In this way you trap air between the two halves. Repeat the movement by lifting the dough again, swing it away from you so that it stretches, slap it onto the table, stretch, then fold it onto itself again. The dough you're working should be oblong; in other words, longer than it is wide. When it starts to be more wide than long, turn it through ninety degrees. Keep working the dough as described at a steady pace, but not too slowly, as this will make the dough stick unnecessarily to your hands and work surface.

After ten to fifteen repetitions, use the scraper to scrape and gather the dough, and shape it into a half-globe shape. The more you practice, the more you will get into the rhythm of working the dough in quick, smooth movements. It is important to relax and not get too frustrated that the dough is sticky. Touch the dough lightly, and work in quick movements. When you have worked the dough sufficiently, it will pay you back by no longer sticking to your hands!

Every time you stretch and fold the dough, you trap air inside it. You will quickly be able to feel that the dough expands and begins to feel silky, smooth, and tight, yet still very much alive . . . like an inflating balloon, slowly expanding.

When you have worked the dough to the stage where it comes cleanly away from the work surface and lets go of your hands, dust the work surface lightly with flour. (This flour will not affect the inner structure of the dough, merely form a dry surface.) Shape the dough into a ball using your scraper. Turn the ball over, and place it top side down into the flour. Stretch and fold all the edges in turn toward the center of the dough, until it makes a nice tight ball. Turn the ball over, and still using your hands, mold and smooth until you have a neat, tight half-globe shape. Place the dough in a lightly floured bowl, put the bowl inside a large plastic bag, close it with a chip clip, and let it rest in a warm place.

4: resting the dough

The most important reasons for resting the dough are:
* to give the yeast cells the opportunity to ferment
* to make sure that the gluten network created during the working of the dough "matures" and is able to stretch optimally, keeping the carbon dioxide (produced by the yeast) within the dough without bursting and collapsing
* to allow enzymes, acids, and by-products from the fermentation (e.g. alcohol) to add flavor to the dough

Even a short resting period allows the yeast cells to work, so the dough increases in size. But if you want to ensure an elastic gluten structure, and improve the aroma of the finished loaf, the rule is this: "Time adds flavor." Long resting periods, cold fermentation, or switching between warm and cold resting periods simply makes better bread. This is the reason that sourdoughs and starters, which have had time to develop, bring extra flavor to the finished bread.

It is important that the dough is resting in a warm place, with 77 to 82°F as the ideal temperature. It is also important to keep the dough away from drafts. You can do this by placing the dough in a large plastic bag (a ten-gallon freezer bag) and closing it with a chip clip or clothespin. The moisture formed during fermentation will lie like dew on the dough's top side, preserving its elasticity and preventing it from drying out. As a rule the dough should double in volume during resting. If the dough is left in a cooler environment, this will take longer. Experience will teach you how to tell when the dough is ready.

It is worth remembering that the extra hours spent on a long fermentation add lots of extra flavor to your breads and make them a lot healthier to eat.

2-4: to mix, work, and rest the dough

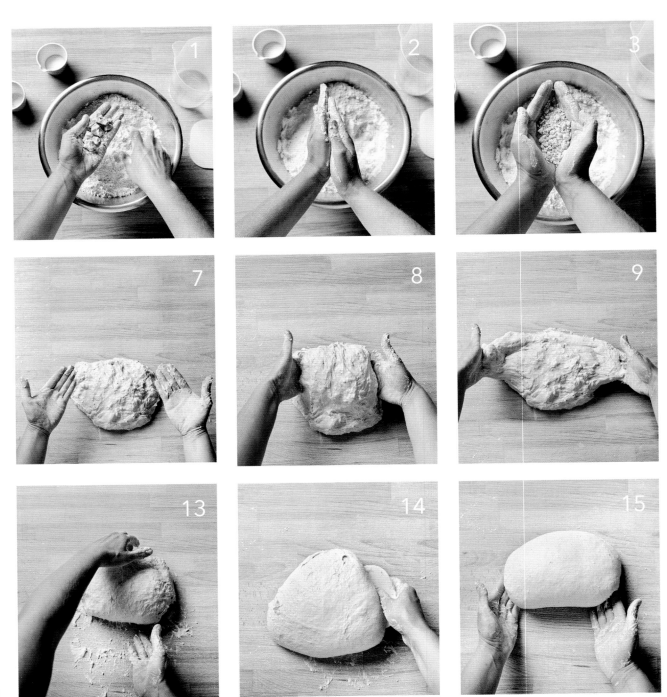

5: dividing the dough

Once the dough is ready, turn it, using your scraper, top side down, out onto a lightly floured work surface. I was originally taught that at this stage you should "knock back" your dough. But you should never be "violent" toward it. Instead, gently press and push with your fingertips to form a rectangle, with the long edge sideways in front of you. This will puncture some of the bubbles that have formed during fermentation. This is called "degassing" the dough. Now fold one third of the dough, along its whole length, in toward the center of the rectangle. Press down along the edge with your fingertips. Repeat from the opposite side. Then fold the dough again, all the way along its length, to form a sausagelike shape. Push the two edges together, forming a seam. Turn the dough over, seam side down. If everything has gone according to plan, you should now be looking at the top side of your dough.

You can now divide the dough into pieces as specified in your recipe. If you are going to divide the dough into many equal-size pieces, such as for rolls, it pays to weigh them out, thus ensuring uniformity, so they will all require the same amount of time in the oven.

Divide the dough up using as few cuts as possible. Each time you cut the dough you wound the gluten network you have created in the dough, and every wound weakens the dough's ability to deliver the perfect result.

6: shaping the dough

In most recipes the final shaping stage of the dough is all about turning it into a tight ball, thereby giving it enough strength and elasticity for the final proofing. In principle the technique used for shaping the dough is the same whether you are working with larger or smaller batches of dough.

To Shape Buns or Rolls
With the top side down, shape into a tight ball by alternately stretching and folding the edges of the dough in toward the center, pressing firmly with your thumb or fingers in turn (see also "Working the Dough,"). Then turn the dough over, and roll it on the work surface, until the bun is tight and smooth.

To Shape Small Oblong Loaves
Shape the dough as if for a bun. Place it top side down, and flatten it into a rough oval shape. Fold one-third of the dough in toward the center, then press down with your fingertips. Fold the opposite third toward the center, and press again. Fold the dough in half along its length, and press down to seal the edges, thereby forming a seam. Now roll the dough back and forth, seam side down, to elongate into a small oblong loaf.

Shaping of Larger Oblong Loaves
Shape the dough into a tight ball (see also "Working the Dough"). Place it top side down, and flatten it into a rough oval shape. Fold one-third of the dough toward the center, then press down with your fingertips. Fold the opposite third toward the center, and press down again. Fold the dough in half along its length, and press down to seal the edges with the heel of your hand, thereby forming a seam. Roll the dough back and forth a couple of times, seam side down, until you have obtained the length you want. If necessary tuck the ends under the dough. Proof the dough in freestanding position, on a sheet pan lined with parchment paper, in a proofing basket, or in a greased loaf pan. Cover the dough with a cloth while proofing.

Shaping of a Large Round Loaf

Place the dough top side down on a floured work surface. Shape into a tight ball (see "Working the Dough"). Turn the ball over, seam side down and top side up, and still using your hands, mold and smooth until you have a neat, tight ball. The dough can proof in freestanding position on a sheet pan covered with parchment paper. If you want to use a proofing basket, the dough should be placed in the floured basket top side down. Cover the dough with a cloth while it is proofing.

7: proofing

In several recipes the dough will rest once for an hour (or until it has doubled in volume) and later proof for forty-five minutes (until nearly doubled in volume). When I rest my dough, the first time around, I am not too particular with timing, apart from acknowledging that a bit more time is always better than too little. However, I am a lot more cautious when I proof the dough. A good rule of thumb is that dough should proof until it has nearly doubled in volume; in other words, when it has expanded to 85 to 90 percent of its original size. If it rises for any longer than that, there is a risk of the dough's collapsing once it goes into the oven. The heat will accelerate yeast activity and therefore also the production of carbon dioxide. For that reason there needs to be enough "stretching room" in the gluten network for it to expand one final time without bursting when it bakes.

It is important that the dough keeps its elasticity and doesn't dry out while proofing. To ensure this I use the large plastic bag again. If this isn't possible because of the size of the dough, I sometimes cover the dough with a cloth and place the plastic bag on top. Temperature is also important; 77 to 82°F is ideal. However, at lower temperatures the dough just needs to proof for a bit longer.

It pays to test the tightness of the dough by gently tapping it with your fingertips. In the beginning it might be difficult to sense when the dough "answers" you in a manner that tells you it is sufficiently proofed. It is even harder for me to try to convey that sensation in words. Only experience counts here, but at some point, with that experience, you will no doubt develop that special "feeling for the dough" that is one of the joys of baking.

8: baking

Before placing your bread in the oven, it pays to gather the equipment you need to work quickly and effectively. Don't forget dusting ingredients for peels and parchment paper, such as coarse cornmeal, which are easily overlooked at this stage. Exact requirements naturally will be influenced by your recipe . . . but an example of essential equipment from several recipes in this book might be a lame with razor blade, peel, coarse cornmeal, and a spray bottle for water.

The razor blade on the little lame is indispensable for scoring the loaf. You use the peel for loading the dough into the oven directly or onto the hot baking stone. Coarse cornmeal acts as "rolling stones," preventing the dough from sticking to the peel. The spray bottle of water is for (generously) misting the oven, as the resulting steam makes the bread more voluminous and gives it a more beautiful color and flavor.

Once you have scored your loaf, it needs to go into the oven immediately. Bear in mind that the heat in the oven decreases dramatically each time you open the door, so the more quickly and efficiently you work when the bread is in the oven, the better.

When soft, moist dough is hit by the heat of the oven, a dramatic physical, biological, and enzymatic change takes place. Once the temperature goes over 140°F, the yeast cells die. Until then the bread keeps rising. At the same time the water in the dough evaporates, creating additional outward pressure in the dough and making the bread rise higher; this is what's known as the "oven spring."

Your bread is fully baked when the core temperature reaches 210°F. You can measure this with your baking thermometer, but experience will quickly teach you to bake with your eye and ear. Look at the color of the bread and the structure of the crust, and teach yourself to recognize the particular hollow sound made by the bread when you tap on its underside with your knuckle. The thermometer will soon become secondary.

9: cooling

When dough is placed in a hot oven, its surface heats up very quickly, but the heat takes a lot longer to penetrate the dough. The same applies in reverse when the bread is taken out of the oven; the crust cools down quickly, and the crumb takes a lot longer to lose its heat. In fact, when the bread is first taken out of the oven, before it has begun to cool down, it actually continues to bake for a while, in the center of the bread, at least. You can demonstrate this by cutting a slice of some just-baked bread; the cut will be uneven, with sticky, pasty bits adhering to the knife. These bits are actually unbaked dough, and they present one of the reasons you should not eat hot bread. Raw dough is not good for the digestion. Another reason for waiting is that you can't actually taste bread when it's still too warm. So even if your whole house smells irresistibly of home baking . . . wait for the bread to cool!

Also remember that bread should cool on a wire rack. If left on the sheet pan, the bread becomes soggy underneath and the crust goes soft.

10: enjoying

Many authors of baking books have written that bread should be eaten in the company of others, and that the word companion, from the Latin *cum pane*, means "someone to share your bread with." Besides the pleasure of sharing with others, I believe you should remember to enjoy your bread with every one of your senses. Smell, taste, texture—and sound! A crispy crust that crunches when you slice the bread brings anticipation for that very first bite.

And did you know that bread can sing?
Some years ago our daughter Marie-Louise worked in a bakery in France. Several times a day batches of baguettes would come out of the large ovens at more or less the same time. Amid all the mayhem one of the bakers would suddenly shout, "Silence! Silence!" Everything would stop, everyone would listen . . . and the baguettes would "sing" as their hot crusts crackled in the relative cool of the bakery air. Much rejoicing—then everyone back to work.

BARLEY, WHEAT, SPELT, AND RYE

BARLEY:
HEALTHY, SWEET,
AND SIX THOUSAND
YEARS OLD

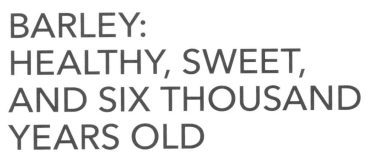

In old Scandinavia the barley
was a heavenly food of the Gods.
Today, it is the "white gold"
of Nordic cuisine.
– Quote from a Skærtoft Mølle flour bag

Scientific Classification
Kingdom: *Plantae* (Plants)
Division: *Angiosperms* (Flowering plants)
Class: *Monocots* (Monocots)
Order: *Poales* (Grass order)
Family: *Poaceae* (Grass family)
Genus: *Hordeum* (Barley)
Species: *Hordeum vulgare*, L.

Next to wheat, barley is the most widely cultivated cereal in Denmark. It is the plant with the longest awn ("beard"), and an old proverb says that it is ready for harvest when the beard turns grey and hangs close to the straw and the barley "sings" or rustles in the sunlight. The plant is a delicate light-green color, the straw is between twenty and thirty-five inches long, and its broad leaves twist clockwise. Barley exists as either hulled or hull-less and as two- or six-row varieties. As with wheat it can be divided into spring barley and winter barley. Breweries usually use spring barley for the malt in their beer production. Most other barley is used for pig fodder. Only a very small proportion of Danish barley gets used for flour or in cooking—but that wasn't always the way. Barley is one of our oldest cereals; imprints of grains in potsherds indicate that it has been present in every prehistoric period, and it is assumed to have been grown in Denmark for more than six thousand years. It was the default grain in bread production until the Renaissance, but when sourdough fermentation became common practice, barley was slowly squeezed out by wheat, which contains much more gluten and thus delivers more voluminous bread. Eventually, over many generations, the "fine" wheat took over completely, reducing barley to the status of a "poor man's food."

Barley has a higher content of essential amino acids than do wheat and rye. It also contains more fiber. During recent years the interest in barley has grown because of its cholesterol-reducing effect. At the same time its central role in the New Nordic Cuisine movement has brought attention to its many gastronomic qualities, and it is now being used more and more in baking and cookery.

WHEAT:
GOLDEN STAR
OF THE WORLD

In the olden days,
rye was foremost . . .
the wheat was kept aside,
for high times and hoedowns.
– Old Danish proverb

Scientific Classification
Kingdom: *Plantae* (Plants)
Division: *Angiosperms* (Flowering plants)
Class: *Monocots* (Monocots)
Order: *Poales* (Grass order)
Family: *Poaceae* (Grass family)
Genus: *Triticum* (Wheat)
Species: *Triticum aestivum*, L.

The wheat we know today is actually a cross between an ancient wheat species and the common goatgrass, known in Danish as "goat-eye" (*Aegilops tauschii*). Around 9,000 BC tribes of the Middle East started cultivating wheat. It began in the country between the Euphrates and the Tigris Rivers, spreading to all the ancient cultures in the area, then on to India, China, and Europe. In Denmark we have grown wheat for about six thousand years, and wheat was introduced into the Americas in the early seventeenth century. Today it is one of the most important sources of nutrition globally and makes up almost 28 percent of all grain production.

There are both winter wheats and spring wheats. In Denmark, as in North America, winter wheat is sown in the autumn and harvested the following summer; spring wheat is sown in the spring and harvested later that year. For wheat that is used in bread baking, protein and gluten content are important. Gluten content depends on the variety chosen by the farmer, along with where, when, and how the grain is grown. To obtain an appropriate gluten content, the growth season has to be warm, with enough water in the soil for the grain to grow; the blooming season sunny; the ripening and harvesting season dry. This will result in gluten-rich wheat, suitable for baking bread.

SPELT: ANCIENT WHEAT WITH A PROMISING FUTURE

Spelt is the better cereal—
warm, rich in nutrition and milder than other grains.
It builds a strong body and healthy blood,
and makes the human spirit warm and happy.
Hildegard of Bingen

Scientific Classification
Kingdom: *Plantae* (Plants)
Division: *Angiosperms* (Flowering plants)
Class: *Monocots* (Monocots)
Order: *Poales* (Grass order)
Family: *Poaceae* (Grass family)
Genus: *Triticum* (Wheat)
Species: *Triticum spelta*, L.

The earliest known species of wheat were einkorn, emmer, and spelt. A growing interest in Nordic gastronomy and indigenous foodstuffs has brought to all of these cereals a well-deserved renaissance; and spelt especially has become very popular. The "ancient wheats" all have a naturally higher content of protein, vitamins, essential amino acids, and minerals than regular wheat. Thus, they make healthier bread with a more pronounced flavor.

Spelt is very suitable for organic production methods. It thrives in both North America and Denmark and produces protein-rich grains with nothing like wheat's demand for fertilizer. Spelt grains are also covered by an extra hull, which makes them more naturally resistant to pests—insects and fungi—than ordinary wheat. However, this does mean that spelt must be dehulled prior to use. This is an energy- and time-consuming process that, along with lower yields, increases the price of the end product.

RYE:
DARK AND BELOVED
IN THE NORTH

On the bottom of the rye kernel is a little picture.

Like a face.

The old called it our Lord's countenance.

But the faces are not alike.

There are just as many different expressions

as with human beings.

Martin A. Hansen

Scientific Classification
Kingdom: *Plantae* (Plants)
Division: *Angiosperms* (Flowering plants)
Class: *Monocots* (Monocots)
Order: *Poales* (Grass order)
Family: *Poaceae* (Grass family)
Genus: *Secale* (Wheat)
Species: *Secale cereale*, L.

Rye is an annual plant that originated in "the Fertile Crescent," an area now comprising the borderlands of Turkey, Iran, Iraq, and Syria.

Ordinary rye is a winter annual, sown in the autumn, that winters as a small, bushy tussock. The leaves are long and thin with sharp edges and a dewy, blue-green color. During the spring the rye forms a flowering shoot with "knees." At the top is the flower (the head), and each flower carries a short "beard." All the pollen seeds within the male flowers ripen at exactly the same time and are released simultaneously. This happens in foglike clouds; we say that the rye is "drifting." This drifting is triggered by changes in light and shadow when a cloud passes over the field. The roots of the rye are deep and may extend as far as seven feet into the ground. The plant grows well in poor soils and withstands the cold better than other cereals; it therefore thrives in the Nordic climate.

The Rye Bread Border

There is a rye bread border across Europe. Scandinavia, the Baltic countries, Poland, North Germany, and Russia all lie north of the border, and this is where the dark, slightly bitter, heavy rye bread is consumed. South of the border, white bread holds sway more or less completely. This border was created as far back as the Iron Age, when a change in climate brought freezing temperatures to the north and made it almost impossible to grow wheat there. Rye was adopted out of bitter necessity in the battle for survival. Two thousand years ago the Roman historian Pliny the Elder wrote of rye that, for the people of the North, it was a "very poor food, good only for avoiding starvation."

Worldwide, the production of rye makes up only 1 percent of total grain production.

RECIPES

Recipes for baking are like love stories: There are only a few originals. The rest—of which there are many—are but variations on the theme!

The spirit of the times, traveling habits, product development . . . all these things put both new and old recipes on the agenda; also health campaigns, TV hosts, and food writers. They inspire and are inspired by the developments taking place on the culinary stage. Just think of how an "old" cereal like barley has recently regained honor and dignity after more than half a century's use as little more than a brewing ingredient, or pig fodder. A renaissance like that would certainly not have occurred without the emergence of the New Nordic Cuisine!

I have collected recipes over a great many years. My collection started when a beloved aunt gave me a fine little notebook, sectioned with tabs that said things like "Starters," "Soups," "Dinner Courses," "Desserts," "Baking," "Cold Cuts," and "Miscellaneous." Since then I have also kept a couple of old shoe boxes and some binders filled with "goodies" from a wide number of baking and cookbooks, food and weekly magazines, all mixed up with pages of handwritten favorite recipes from friends. And then there are all the experiments that have come along since we started working with grain and flour at Skærtoft.

My recipes, which have all been adjusted to suit both the French way of working the dough and the stone-ground flour, are a lovely jumble of breads and pastries with one thing in common: I like them. A lot of my recipes are healthy and rich in fiber. But healthy is only good if it is also tasty! Besides, in my opinion life is far too short to leave out something for the sweet tooth.

Diversity: That's what keeps life exciting. And this applies to baking, too!

All lovely things are also necessary.
John Ruskin

BAKING
WITH YEAST

Before you start making dough, it is a good idea to gather all the necessary ingredients on your table and allow them to warm to room temperature. If this isn't possible, then assess whether any cooler components, such as cold flour, a cold bowl, or cold eggs, might demand slightly warmer water. Similarly, on a hot summer's day, the liquid might need to be a little cooler than normal. A cold kitchen is no good for either making or resting dough. If there is no time to heat the room, then help your dough by adjusting the water temperature accordingly.

Nonorganic yeast thrives at a dough temperature of about 77°F. Organic yeast, which ferments a little more slowly, prefers things a little warmer and thrives really well at 82°F. At temperatures below 50°F or above 115°F, the yeast works noticeably slower, and it dies when the temperature goes over 140°F.

When you use good-quality stone-ground flour, it is not necessary to add sugar to your dough by default to maximize fermentation. Stone-ground flour has a sufficiently high natural sugar content to activate the yeast.

"Flour, water, yeast and salt! Mix it, work the dough and bake it—and you have a bread that in many ways will outcompete the breads you can buy." This quote from Richard Bertinet is the essence of my many stays at the Bertinet Kitchen in England. It is that simple, appealing, and fun. To Richard's words I would like to add that with these four ingredients you are not limited to making only one type of bread. You have the potential to diversify as much as you like when you shape and bake your dough—if you let your imagination run riot. This bread is a very traditional basket bread with a crosslike cut on the top, a reminder of times when the cross symbolized a crucifix, keeping evils away from the essential bread making.

THE BASIC LOAF

Equipment: 2.2-lb (1-kg) proofing basket

10 g fresh yeast
500 g sifted wheat or spelt flour
10 g salt
Approx. 350 g water

Rub the yeast into the flour, and add the salt and water. Mix and work the dough as shown in steps 2–4 on pages 48–49, then let it rest until it has doubled in volume.

Turn the dough out onto a floured work surface and degas slightly. Fold and shape the dough into a ball, and place top side down in a floured proofing basket. Leave to proof until it has nearly doubled in volume.

Preheat the convection oven, with baking stone, to 480°F.

Turn the loaf out onto a baking peel dusted with coarse cornmeal. Score the loaf. Then, using a spray bottle, generously mist the inside of the oven with water. Ease the loaf onto the baking stone; spray a little more water into the oven before closing the oven door.

After 5 minutes, lower the temperature to 410°F, and bake for 20 to 25 minutes more.

In Heiligkreuztal in Germany, south of Stuttgart, you'll find the family business of Adelinde and Karl-Heinz Häussler. It's an interesting company, specializing in stone ovens. Back in the 1960s, when Karl-Heinz was the village blacksmith, the area was hit by a vicious hurricane. For many days the village was without power, and Adelinde could not cook any hot meals. It was a bad situation and an experience she never wanted to repeat. So Karl-Heinz went to the smithy and produced his first wood-fired stove and oven for Adelinde. Since then, both stove and oven have become the center of a flourishing business, exporting to most of the world . . . and Adelinde is queen, not just of her own kitchen, but also of the Häussler Baking School. It is from her that I got the inspiration for this bread.

CONVENT BREAD

Equipment: 2.2-lb (1-kg) couronne proofing basket

40 g sesame seeds
40 g sunflower seeds
350 g sifted wheat flour
75 g whole-wheat rye flour
75 g sifted spelt flour
10 g fresh yeast
10 g salt
Approx. 425 g buttermilk

Toast the seeds lightly in a dry frying pan.

Mix the three types of flour thoroughly, and rub the yeast into the flour. Then add the remaining ingredients.

Mix and work the dough as shown in steps 2–4 on pages 48–49. Leave the dough to rest for 1 hour, then degas it slightly, shape it into a ball, and leave it to rest for another hour or until it has doubled in volume.

Turn the dough out onto a floured work surface. Divide into two equal-size halves, shape them into balls, cover with a cloth, and leave them to rest for 10 minutes.

Then shape into two long sausage shapes, twist the "strands" together, and place them in the floured couronne. Make sure the ends are well joined. Leave the loaf to proof until it has nearly doubled in volume.

Preheat the convection oven, with baking stone, to 480°F.

Turn the loaf out onto a baking peel dusted with coarse cornmeal. Then, using a spray bottle, generously mist the inside of the oven with water. Ease the bread onto the baking stone; spray a little more water into the oven. Repeat after 1 minute. After 5 minutes of baking, lower the temperature to 390°F and bake the bread for another 30 to 40 minutes.

Anton, Gitte, and Bo from Gilleleje came visiting on a grey and tedious vacation day. The weather on our island of Als was nothing to celebrate, so how about a spontaneous visit to our mill? I had a long chat with Gitte and Bo about flour, health issues, and good bread—definitely too long for Anton's liking. He is eight and on vacation, so it is probably not flour that rocks his world. A week later we received an e-mail from Gitte, thanking us for the visit and including the recipe for Anton's Favorite Loaf, which these days is one of our favorites, too. I hope Anton has forgiven us!

ANTON'S FAVORITE BREAD

25 g sesame seeds
175 g sifted wheat flour
100 g whole-rye flour
225 g durum flour
10 g fresh yeast
10 g salt
50 g white poppy seeds
50 g (approx. 2½ tbsp) maple syrup
250 g buttermilk
20 g (approx. 2 tbsp) sesame oil
Approx. 110 g water

Toast the sesame seeds in a dry frying pan.

Mix the different flour types and rub in the yeast. Then add the remaining ingredients, and mix and work the dough as described previously. Let the dough rest for 2 hours or until it has doubled in volume. It can also rest in the fridge overnight, if the amount of yeast is reduced to 5 g.

Turn the dough out onto a floured work surface. Degas slightly; fold and shape into an oblong loaf. Place on a sheet pan lined with parchment paper. Cover with a cloth, and leave to proof until nearly doubled in volume.

Preheat the oven to 390°F.

When the dough is ready, sprinkle it with whole-rye flour, then score the loaf. Using a spray bottle, generously mist the inside of the oven with water. Place the loaf on the second shelf up and spray a little more water into the oven. Bake for 45 to 50 minutes.

Inger is the sister of mine who can bake. She is especially good at pastries but is also a dab hand at coarse bread. One of her creations in the genre is this delightful seed bread, named after the village in which she lives. The first time she made the bread it was for a neighbor, who does not eat rye bread but still enjoys a coarse bread. I find that this bread, which stays delicious for several days, is a nice supplement at the lunch table, especially for cold cuts and mild cheese . . . or even eaten quite simply, with just a little cold butter.

FREDERIKSGÅRD LUNCH BREAD

Equipment: ½-gallon (1½-liter) loaf pan

250 g whole-spelt flour
250 g sifted spelt flour
20 g fresh yeast
10 g salt
50 g pine nuts
70 g pumpkin seeds
100 g sunflower seeds
275 g plain yogurt
20 g (approx. 1 tbsp) olive oil
Approx. 275 g whole milk

For brushing:
A little melted butter in warm water

Decoration:
Pine nuts, pumpkin and sunflower seeds

Mix the two types of flour. Rub in the yeast and add the remaining ingredients. Mix the dough thoroughly. This dough only needs mixing and should have the consistency of a thick porridge.

Place the dough into a buttered loaf pan, and smooth its top. Let it rest for 1 hour.

Melt the butter in the warm water. Brush the surface of the loaf, then decorate with mixed seeds. Score the loaf just before placing the pan in the center of a cold oven.

Set the oven at 340°F, and bake the bread for 1¼ to 1½ hours.

Once baked, it should be left in the pan and covered with a cloth. After 10 minutes, remove it from the pan, wrap it in the cloth, and leave it to cool on a wire rack.

I have an abundance of ramsons, or wild garlic, in my garden. It thrives below the beech trees on the border of my rhododendron bed, and in May and June its leaves and flowers adorn my salad bowls, herb meatballs, and bread. Later in the summer I use the little unripe fruit buds as capers or preserve them in syrup with pearls of rye, barley, or spelt and fruits of blackthorn or sea buckthorn. The recipe for the preserved pearls was created by chef Andreas Hartvig, but the recipe for this bread is entirely my own!

COCOTTE BREAD WITH RAMSONS

Equipment: stoneware cocotte, or Dutch oven for 4.4 lb (2-kg) of dough

700 g sifted spelt flour
300 g whole-spelt flour
7 g fresh yeast
20 g salt
80 g chopped hazelnuts
10 g finely cut ramsons leaves, or chives,
rosemary, thyme—whichever is in season
500 g dark, nutty-tasting beer
20 g (1 tbsp) neutral oil
Approx. 200 g lukewarm water

Mix the two flour types thoroughly, and rub the yeast into the flour. Add the remaining ingredients, then mix and work the dough as shown in steps 2–4 on pages 48–49. Let it rest overnight in a cool place, or in the fridge.

Remove the dough from the fridge, and let it warm on the kitchen table for a couple of hours.

Grease the cocotte—both top and bottom—thoroughly with oil.

Turn the dough out onto a floured work surface. Degas slightly; fold and shape into a round loaf, and place it in the bottom half of the cocotte. Push the dough gently to make it fill out the cocotte. Leave the cocotte and dough, without the "lid" on, to proof for 1 hour, or until the dough has nearly doubled in volume.

Score the loaf, put the cocotte "lid" on, and place it on a sheet pan on the second shelf up, in a cold oven.

Set the temperature at 390°F, and bake for 1½ hours.

Remove from the cocotte immediately, and leave to cool on a wire rack.

Many years ago, during a holiday in France, I was served a couple of slices of rustic farm bread, which had a wonderful light taste and a fragrance of lavender. Every slice of bread was generously covered with a soft and creamy goat cheese, and it was served with a little sprinkling of lavender flowers and a dish of black olives. I enjoyed every mouthful immensely and have tried with this recipe to capture my memories of a beautiful summer lunch in Provence. I would definitely recommend the combination of goat cheese and olives with the bread and also—naturally—a glass of fine red wine.

LAVENDER BREAD

Equipment: 2.2-lb (1-kg) round proofing basket

10 g fresh yeast
350 g sifted spelt flour
150 g whole-spelt flour
10 g salt
30 g (1½ tbsp) fluid honey
2 g (1 tsp) dried lavender flowers
Approx. 350 g lukewarm water

Rub the yeast into the flour, then add the remaining ingredients. Mix and work the dough as shown in steps 2-4 on pages 48-49. Let it rest for 30 minutes. Turn it out onto a floured work surface; degas slightly. Shape it into a ball, put it back in the bowl, and let it rest until it has doubled in volume.

Preheat the convection oven, with baking stone, to 480°F.

Turn the dough out onto a floured work surface, and degas slightly. Fold and shape it into a round loaf, and place it, top side down, in a floured proofing basket. Leave to proof until it has nearly doubled in volume.

Turn the dough out onto a baking peel dusted with coarse cornmeal. Score the loaf. Then, using a spray bottle, generously mist the inside of the oven with water. Ease the bread onto the baking stone and spray a little more water into the oven. Immediately lower the heat to 410°F.

Bake the bread for 25 to 35 minutes.

Hanne Bonde lives in Helved, a cozy little village not far from Skaertoft. Hanne works at a day care facility, and loves to bake with "her kids." She is often disturbed by the fact that so many children dislike vegetables, so she does whatever she can to smuggle healthy stuff and "greens" into their food without their noticing. The result is often some really yummy recipes, such as this one. The children love these vegetable buns—especially, according to Hanne, as a little "meal between meals."

VEGETABLE BREAD AND BUNS

Makes 2 loaves; 32 to 35 buns
Equipment: 2.2-lb (1-kg) round proofing baskets

20 g fresh yeast
500 g sifted spelt flour
500 g whole-spelt flour
20 g salt
1 large egg
200 g finely grated carrot
10 g (approx. 1 cup) chopped parsley
100 g (approx. 5 tbsp) rapeseed oil
300 g vegetable juice
Approx. 300 g water

For brushing:
1 egg, whipped with a little cold water

Rub the yeast into the flour, and add the remaining ingredients. Mix and work the dough as shown in steps 2–4 on pages 48–49, and leave it to rest for 30 minutes.

Turn the dough out onto a floured work surface. Degas it slightly, shape it into a ball, and put it back into the bowl; let it rest for another 30 minutes or until it's doubled in volume.

Preheat the convection oven, with baking stone, to 480°F.

Turn the dough out onto a floured work surface, and degas slightly. Fold and shape the dough into a round loaf (or buns, if desired) and place, top side down, into a dusted proofing basket. Leave to proof until nearly doubled in volume.

Turn the loaf out onto a baking peel dusted with coarse cornmeal. Brush the top with egg, and score the loaf. Generously mist the inside of the oven with water. Ease the bread onto the baking stone, and spray a little more water into the oven. Immediately lower the temperature to 410°F.

Bake for 30 to 40 minutes.

The 60-g buns should bake for approximately 20 minutes at 430°F.

APRICOT BREAD
IN A RÖMERTOPF

Equipment: Römertopf or other cocotte

Before I got my stoneware cocottes from the ceramist Sigrid Hovmand on the Island of Samsø, I sometimes used an old-fashioned Römertopf for baking. I have three different ones: one for meat, one for fish, and one for bread. They do not last forever, and over the years I have had to buy new ones. Every time I do, I feel a little downhearted. I love the patina that develops with use on the porous clay, a patina that reflects the delicious results I get, regardless of which one of my three 'Topfs I use.

10 g fresh yeast
350 g sifted wheat flour
10 g salt
10 g light cane sugar
A little finely grated nutmeg
10 g (½ tbsp) neutral oil
Approx. 250 g water
100 g coarsely chopped dried apricots

Rub the yeast into the flour. Add the remaining ingredients—except the apricots—and mix and work the dough as shown in steps 2-4 on pages 48-49.

When the dough is worked, press it out into a square shape. Spread onto this the chopped apricots. Fold the dough, and shape it into a ball. Leave to rest until it's doubled in volume.

While the dough is resting, place the porous clay cocotte (both halves) into cold water for a minimum of 10 minutes. Remove it from the water, wipe it dry, then oil the insides.

When the dough is ready, turn it out onto a floured work surface. Degas slightly, then fold and shape into an oblong loaf, which should fit into the Römertopf. Place it in the bottom half of the Römertopf; cover with a cloth. Leave to proof for 45 minutes.

Put the lid on, and place the 'Topf in a cold oven. Set the temperature to 390°F. Approximately 1¼ hours later the bread is finished. Remove from the Römertopf immediately, and leave it to cool on a wire rack.

By adding both dried and fresh fruit to the dough, you change the taste and texture of the finished bread. Only through experimentation will your favorite mix of fruits reveal itself. Here I have chosen to let the acidity of the buttermilk and the tartness of the apple "talk" to the concentrated sweetness of the dried dates.

APPLE-DATE BREAD

Equipment: 2.2-lb (1-kg) round proofing basket

300 g sifted spelt flour
75 g whole-spelt flour
125 g durum flour
10 g fresh yeast
10 g salt
Approx. 250 g lukewarm water
100 g buttermilk
100 g tart, firm apples, finely cubed
100 g dried dates, finely cubed

Mix the three types of flour thoroughly. Rub the yeast into the flour, and add the salt, water, and buttermilk. Mix and work the dough as described previously until the dough is nearly done. Then add the cubed apples and dates, finish the dough, and let it rest until it has doubled in volume.

Preheat the oven to 390°F.

Gently turn the dough out onto a floured work surface. Degas slightly; fold and shape the dough into a round loaf and place, top side down, in a floured proofing basket. Let it proof until nearly doubled in volume.

Turn the loaf out onto a sheet pan lined with parchment paper. Score the loaf; place the pan in the center of the oven. Bake for 40 to 45 minutes.

Some nutritionists are full of praise for the health benefits of the potato (depending on the person). It is rich in complex carbohydrates, which, with their slow-release energy, suit many bodies well. The potato has a low fat content but large amounts of protein, calcium, iron, potassium, zinc, and vitamins. I find potatoes very tasty indeed—and also when used in bread. They bring a soft and spongy feel to the crumb and make the bread stay fresh for ages.

POTATO BREAD

250 g cooked, dry potatoes
30 g butter
Approx. 500 g hot water from
the cooked potatoes
100 g whole-rye flour
20 g fresh yeast
900 g sifted wheat flour
200 g plain yogurt
15 g salt
5 g (1 tbsp) ground fennel seeds
20 g (1 tbsp) grade B maple syrup

For brushing:
A little yogurt mixed with water

Peel the potatoes and cook them. Mash them with butter and leave to cool.

Pour the hot potato water onto the whole-rye flour, mix, and leave to cool.

Rub the yeast into the wheat flour. Mix the yogurt with the rye flour/water mix, and add all other ingredients. Mix and work the dough as shown in steps 2–4 on pages 48–49, then let it rest for 1 to 1½ hours, or until it has doubled in volume.

Remove some of the dough to make the decorative braid with; divide this into three equal pieces, fold and shape them into long strands, and make into a braid. Shape the larger portion of dough into an oblong loaf, brush a little water down its back, then stick down the braid. Let it proof, on a sheet pan lined with parchment paper, until the loaf has nearly doubled in volume.

Preheat the oven to 350°F.

Brush the loaf with some yogurt mixed with a little water, place on the second shelf up, and bake for 60 to 80 minutes.

The national sport in the southern part of Denmark is an unusual one called "Ring Riding." Every weekend throughout the summer, horses of every size, shape, and color are steered in a slow canter toward a "gallows," where a tiny ring is suspended, which the contestants, or "tilters," are supposed to spear with their lances. It may look easy, but believe me, it's not!

We have a few large Ring Riding competitions in the area with several hundred riders, big, showy events with thousands of spectators. And then there are the many smaller events, without the commercial glamour but with genuine, local roots. One of them takes place in Frydendal: six gallows, eighty horses, a tombola, a beer tent, and plenty of traditional Ring Riding franks—including freshly baked buns made by Ulla. It's a great event! Every summer, the second weekend in July.

BUNS FOR TILTERS

Makes 15 to 18 buns
Equipment: springform pan, 10 inches across

500 g sifted spelt flour
50 g barley flakes or rolled oats
40 g fresh yeast
10 g salt
20 g (1 tbsp) honey
1 large egg
100 g tart, roughly grated apple
150 g milk
Approx. 150 g lukewarm water

Mix the flour and barley flakes/oats. Rub the yeast into the flour mixture, and add the remaining ingredients. Mix and work the dough as shown in steps 2–4 on pages 48–49, then let it rest until it has almost doubled in volume.

Turn the dough onto a floured work surface. Degas slightly, then fold and make into a sausage shape. Cut into 60-g pieces, and shape into buns. Place the buns in the greased springform pan, spaced slightly apart but in the overall pattern of a flower. Let them proof until they just about fill the pan.

Preheat the oven to 390°F.

Brush the buns with egg wash, and decorate with barley flakes or rolled oats.

Generously mist the inside of the oven with water. Place the springform pan on a sheet pan on the second shelf up. Bake the buns for approximately 40 minutes. When they are done, open the springform and carefully ease the "flower" onto a wire rack. Leave the buns to cool entirely before gently breaking apart the flower.

Buns can be baked separately at 360°F, for approximately 15 minutes.

Thriftiness is probably the reason that this classic mix of sifted wheat and sifted rye was invented. The expensive wheat was "stretched out," so to speak, with the much cheaper rye. The blending proportions vary, but I believe that 60 percent wheat and 40 percent sifted rye is the most common mix. This particular bread has a characteristically soft, slightly moist crumb, and a beautiful crust turned dark brown and sweet by the malt syrup.

OLD-FASHIONED SYRUP BREAD

Equipment: approx. 1-gallon (2½- to 3-liter) loaf pan

350 g sifted wheat flour
150 g sifted rye flour
5 g fresh yeast
10 g salt
175 g buttermilk
40 g (approx. 2 tbsp) malt syrup
Approx. 175 g water

For brushing:
A little melted butter in warm water

Mix the two types of flour. Rub in the yeast; add the remaining ingredients, then mix and work the dough as shown in steps 2–4 on pages 48–49. Let the dough rest in the fridge for 10 to 12 hours or overnight.

Take the dough from the fridge. Degas it slightly, shape the dough into a ball, put it back in the bowl, and let it rest for approximately 4 hours at room temperature.

Turn the dough out onto a floured work surface, degas slightly, and shape into an oblong loaf. Place in the loaf pan. Let the loaf proof for 3 hours until the dough almost reaches the top of the pan.

Preheat the oven to 440°F.

Prick the loaf, and brush with melted butter. Place the loaf pan on a sheet pan in the center of the oven. Bake the bread for 30 to 35 minutes. If the top of the loaf turns too dark during baking, cover it with aluminum foil for the remainder of the baking time.

When the loaf is baked, it should be left in the pan for 10 minutes before it's removed and allowed to cool completely.

Cranberries are commonplace today, easily obtained in any super-market, so it's easy to forget that this sweet-sour berry wasn't widely available until quite recently. More of a Nordic than a Danish berry, the cranberry has many qualities, including antioxidants and a very high vitamin C content. In the old days they were used to prevent inflam-mation of the bladder and scurvy. I find that the tartness of the cranberries adds a pleasant edge to the taste of this bread, working off the soft barley flakes and the sweetness of the honey.

WHEAT BREAD WITH CRANBERRIES

Equipment: 2.2-lb (1-kg) couronne proofing basket

400 g sifted wheat flour
100 g barley flakes
5 g fresh yeast
10 g salt
10 g (approx. ½ tbsp) liquid honey
Approx. 350 g water
50 g dried, sweet cranberries

Mix the flour and the barley flakes. Rub in the yeast and add the salt, honey, and water. Mix and work the dough as shown in steps 2–4 on pages 48–49. Just before the dough is done, add the cranberries; finish the dough and leave to rest for 1 hour. After 1 hour, slightly degas, shape into a ball, and leave to rest again. Repeat after 1 hour, then leave until it has nearly doubled in volume.

Turn the dough out onto a floured work surface; degas slightly. Fold and shape into a sausage shape; place it in the floured proofing basket. Remember to join the ends. Leave to proof until nearly doubled in volume.

Preheat the convection oven, with baking stone, to 480°F.

Turn the loaf out onto a baking peel dusted with coarse cornmeal. Generously mist the inside of the oven with water. Ease the bread onto the baking stone; spray a little more water into the oven. Repeat after 30 seconds. After 5 minutes, lower the oven to 410°F. Bake for another 25 to 35 minutes.

Many years ago the chef Andreas Hartvig showed me some dough he was preparing in his mixer. The regular dough hook and low, steady speed had been replaced by a very high-speed whisk. But if this whipping seemed rough, the care and attention with which he then worked the dough was every bit as gentle as the regular hook. . . and the result was a light, delicious loaf, with a moist crumb and a thin, crunchy crust.

WHIPPED BREAD

Makes 2 loaves
Equipment: mixer

840 g sifted spelt flour
160 g whole-spelt flour
10 g fresh yeast
20 g salt
Approx. 800 g water

Mix the two types of flour in the mixing bowl, rub in the yeast, and add the salt and water. Mix the dough at high speed using a whisk until the dough no longer sticks to the sides and bottom of the bowl. Scrape the soft dough off the whisk, put a lid on the mixing bowl, and let the dough rest in the fridge overnight.

The next day, allow the dough to warm for a couple of hours before continuing.

Gently turn the dough out onto a generously floured work surface, and dust the top of the dough with a little flour. Divide the dough into four equal-size pieces. Quickly twist the pieces together in pairs, preserving as much air in the dough as possible. Place the two twisted loaves on separate peels lined with parchment paper. Let them proof until nearly doubled in volume.

Preheat the convection oven, with baking stone, to 480°F.

Generously mist the inside of the oven with water. Ease the loaves, along with the parchment paper, onto the baking stone. Spray a little more water into the oven. Repeat after 1 minute.

After 5 minutes of baking, lower the heat to 410°F, then bake the loaves for another 20 to 30 minutes more.

When we first started polishing, cutting, and kibbling grains, it seemed natural to start experimenting with new possibilities in both cooking and baking. Our pearls—whole, polished grains of spelt, barley, and rye—are hard to beat in cooking, while the cut and cracked grains add something really special to bread. "Mouthfeel," the way food's textures are experienced in the mouth, is of increasing interest to people studying food and the senses. In bread, cut and cracked grains add a whole new structure to the crumb and give it "bite"—mouthfeel at its best.

CRACKED RYE BREAD RINGS

Makes 2 loaves
Equipment: a cookie cutter, 2 to 2.5 inches across

75 g cracked rye
Approx. 200 g water
425 g sifted wheat flour
100 g sifted rye flour
20 g fresh yeast
15 g salt
20 g (1 tbsp) olive oil
300 g dark beer

For brushing:
10 g sifted rye flour
50 g beer

Cook the cracked rye in the water for a couple of minutes and let it cool. Mix the two types of flour thoroughly, and rub in the yeast. Add the softened grains, water, and remaining ingredients. Mix and work the dough until it feels smooth and elastic.

Let it rest for 2 to 3 hours or until it has almost doubled in volume.

Turn the dough out onto a floured work surface, and degas it gently. Divide the dough, and shape into two large round loaves, 7 to 8 inches across. Sprinkle a little whole-rye flour or cracked rye on a sheet pan lined with parchment paper. Place the loaves on the pan, and cut a hole in the middle of each one using the cookie cutter. Leave the loaves to proof until they have nearly doubled in volume.

Preheat the oven to 440°F.

For the brushing: parboil the sifted rye in the beer.

Prick the bread rings, brush them with the rye flour/beer mix, and place them in the center of the oven. Bake for 10 minutes, then lower the heat to 360°F, and bake for 30 to 40 minutes more. Cool on a wire rack before eating.

Pâtisserie and fine pastry: In my childhood just those words would always make our mouths water. We rarely had it; only on special occasions, really, because my mother baked everything herself. Every day, and in increasing amounts, she would bake this bread. As we began to grow up and bring home friends both for afternoon get-togethers and for dinners, a single loaf never lasted long, so she baked two of them every single day, and in the spirit of that age, her loaves were as fine and soft as this whole milk bread.

WHOLE MILK BREAD

10 g fresh yeast
60 g room-temperature butter
500 g sifted wheat flour
10 g salt
10 g (approx. 2 tsp) light cane sugar
Approx. 350 g lukewarm whole milk

For brushing:
1 egg
A little milk

Rub the yeast and butter into the flour. Add remaining ingredients, then mix and work the dough as shown in steps 2–4 on pages 48–49. Let it rest until it's doubled in volume.

Turn the dough out onto a floured work surface, and degas slightly. Divide into three equal pieces, then fold and shape into balls. Let them rest on the table for 10 minutes, under a cloth.

Shape the three balls into sausage shapes, and braid them into a loaf. Make sure the ends are well joined. Place on a sheet pan lined with parchment paper. Cover, and leave to proof until the loaf is nearly doubled in volume.

Preheat the oven to 390°F.

Beat the egg and milk. Use to brush the loaf, then bake it on the second shelf up for 40 to 45 minutes.

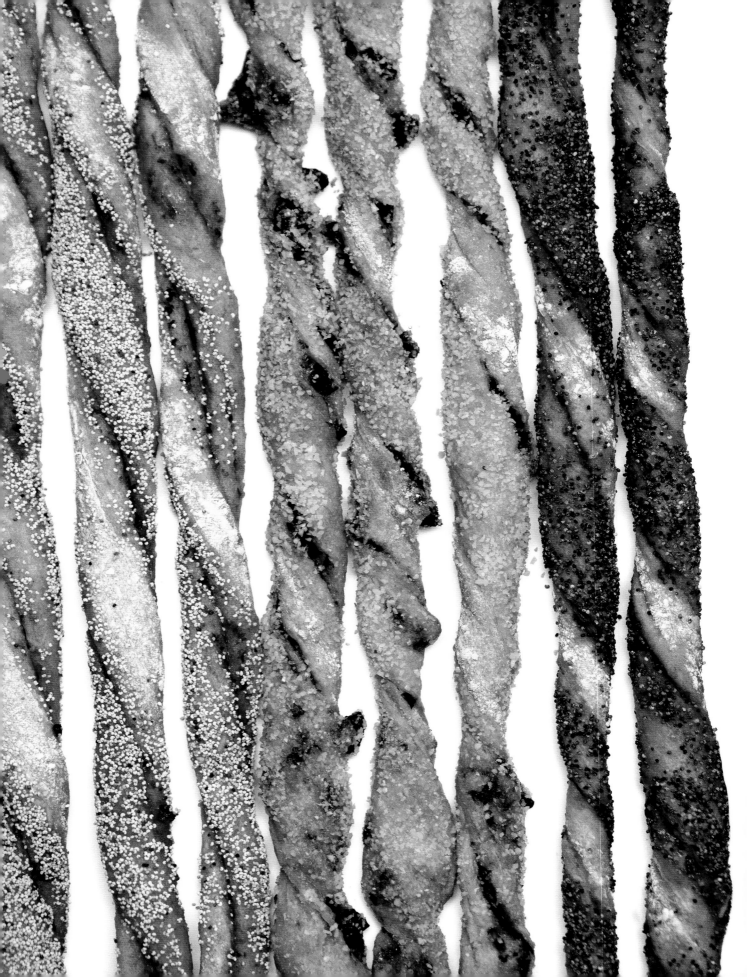

If you are tired of serving chips, peanuts, and pistachios with your welcome drinks, then here is a really nice alternative: deliciously crunchy, tasty breadsticks, which are at their best when served straight from the oven. You needn't stress about preparing them, because you can easily make them in advance, prebake them about two-thirds of the way, cool them, then bake them just prior to serving. The first time I tasted breadsticks was during one of my stays with Richard Bertinet. These days I have several variations on the original theme . . . however, the three types below are my family's favorites.

BREADSTICKS

Makes 30 to 34 sticks

350 g sifted wheat or spelt flour
150 g whole-wheat or whole-spelt flour
10 g fresh yeast
10 g salt
Approx. 350 g water

Filling and decoration suggestions:
Basil or arugula pesto and finely grated Parmesan. Rolled in blue poppy seeds.
Red pesto and finely grated Parmesan. Rolled in white poppy seeds.
Finely chopped olives and finely grated Parmesan. Rolled in coarse cornmeal.

Mix the two types of flour thoroughly, rub in the yeast, and add the salt and water. Mix and work the dough as shown in steps 2–4 on pages 48–49. Let it rest until it has doubled in volume.

Preheat the convection oven, with baking stone, to 480°F.

Turn the dough out onto a floured work surface, and flatten into a rectangle. Cut it into three equal rectangles, and spread on the three different fillings, one on each.

Fold a third of the dough into the center; then fold the opposite side over on top, all the way across. Press gently onto the "closed" dough with your palms, working the filling into the dough. Repeat for the other two varieties.

Cut the rectangle lengthwise with your scraper into 0.2- to 0.3-inch-wide strips. Pick each one up in turn, twisting and stretching it to a length of approximately 11 inches (or the length of your baking tray). Roll each one in its respective seeds/decorations before placing onto a sheet pan lined with parchment paper or, alternatively, onto non-stick trays. Bake them as soon as the tray is filled. If you let them proof, they will be more like bread and less like a "crunchy snack"! Bake for 10 to 12 minutes if the strips are thin, a little longer if they turned out thicker.

I am a real nerd when it comes to bread rolls. The thing is, I just love to serve small, delicious rolls when we have visitors. Naturally, the rolls must taste fantastic . . . but they must also be beautiful to look at—differently shaped, colored, and decorated—because, as everyone knows, we also eat with our eyes. The fact that these rolls make a perfect little snack between meals, or fit easily into a lunch box, is an extra bonus!

LITTLE LEMON ROLLS

Makes approx. 16 rolls

425 g sifted wheat flour
75 g whole-rye flour
10 g fresh yeast
10 g salt
Grated zest from 1 lemon
Approx. 350 g lukewarm water

Decoration:
Coarse cornmeal

Mix the two types of flour, and rub the yeast into the flour, then add the salt, lemon zest, and water. Mix and work the dough as shown in steps 2-4 on pages 48-49. Let it rest until it has doubled in volume.

Turn the dough out onto a floured work surface, and degas slightly. Fold and shape the dough into a sausage shape approximately 2.75 inches in diameter. Moisten your palms in a little oil, spread the oil onto the dough, then roll it in the coarse cornmeal until it is covered.

Divide the dough—with single cuts, using a metal dough cutter—into 1-inch slices. Place the slices on a sheet pan lined with parchment paper, with the smooth cuts facing upward. Cover and leave to proof until they have nearly doubled in volume.

Preheat the convection oven to 480°F.

Generously mist the inside of the oven with water. Place the rolls in the center of the oven. Spray a little more water into the oven, then lower the heat to 430°F. Bake for approximately 15 minutes, until the rolls turn a beautiful golden color.

Some years ago I took part in a nature-film festival in France, where I showed a film about that mysterious, wary, elusive bird, the bittern. The festival was held in an incredibly diverse bird environment, not far from the Atlantic coast and the Île de Ré, where they produce the best sea salt I have ever tasted. The gathering was also used to mark the beginning of a campaign: to save the stinging nettle in France! It came as a surprise to me that the stinging nettle is endangered there, but it turns out that, within the French landscape, modern agriculture has all but managed to kill it off completely. So a loud, clear Gallic battle cry was being sounded—with gastronomy as one of the many weapons. The "green knots" used in the campaign won my heart . . . the bittern won the hearts of the film jury . . . and the film won a prize.

GREEN KNOTS

Makes approx. 10 knots

300 g sifted wheat flour
50 g whole-wheat flour
15 g fresh yeast
25 g unsalted butter
10 g salt
1 large egg, lightly beaten
50 g, or 2 cups, of fresh, finely chopped stinging nettle top-leaves; alternatively, you can use 2 tbsp of dried stinging nettles
Approx. 200 g whole milk

For brushing:
1 egg, beaten with a little milk
Some good-quality flaked sea salt

Mix the two types of flour, rub in the yeast and butter, add the rest of the ingredients, then mix and work the dough as shown in steps 2-4 on pages 48-49. Leave the dough to rest until it has nearly doubled in volume.

Turn the dough out onto a floured work surface. Fold and shape into a sausage shape. Cut into pieces of 70 g each. Shape them into little balls, and let them rest under a cloth for 10 minutes.

You make each knot in the following way: Flatten the ball, fold it twice, and roll it into a long sausage shape. Tie the ends into a simple knot, leaving a fair amount of space at the center. Tuck the topmost end under, then take the lowermost end over the top of the dough and "thread it" through the center. Tuck both ends neatly underneath the dough, and finish off into a ring shape. Put the knots onto a sheet pan lined with parchment paper, and allow to proof until nearly doubled in size.

Preheat the convection oven to 480°F.

Brush the knots with the beaten egg. Sprinkle with some sea salt flakes, and place them in the center of the oven. Bake for approximately 15 minutes.

In my baking library there are two books by American writers whom I appreciate immensely and who have taught me a great deal: Jeffrey Hamelman and Peter Reinhart. Both of them tell delightful stories about their lives in bread baking and the inspiring bakers they have met over the years; for instance, the grand old man of baking, Philippe Gosselin from Paris. For his famous "Pains à l'Ancienne," he uses a special method in which the fermentation of the dough is prolonged using ice-cold water, thus enhancing the flavor of the bread. This technique has gained him world recognition. Last time I searched the Internet for "Pains à l'Ancienne," there were 657,000 hits for this one particular bread. It may be a little difficult to work with, but it pays off to give it a chance. The taste is fantastic!

PAINS À L'ANCIENNE

Makes 6 loaves
Equipment: mixer, baking pan

Approx. 550 g ice-cold water
10 g fresh yeast
750 g sifted wheat or spelt flour
15 g salt

Put your water in the fridge a couple of hours before making the dough. Immediately before use, cool the water even further by adding a handful of ice cubes.

Rub the yeast into the flour in the mixing bowl and add the salt and ice-cold water (add more ice-cold water to the dough if it feels too compact). Mix the dough thoroughly until it no longer sticks to the sides and bottom of the mixing bowl and remains more or less completely on the dough hook. This dough *must* be very soft and moist when it is done. Scrape the dough into an oiled bowl, cover the bowl with plastic wrap, and place in the fridge overnight.

The next day, leave the dough to warm on the kitchen table for 2 to 3 hours. When it has doubled in volume, dust the work surface with flour. Then, gently turn the dough out onto the surface. You can dip your metal dough cutter in water to prevent the dough from sticking to it. Try to avoid degassing the dough. If the dough is very wet, dust it with a little flour. If the dough sticks to the surface, lift it very gently and dust some flour beneath it.

Carefully shape the dough into a rectangle of 6 x 8 inches. If the dough becomes difficult to handle, dust it with flour. Divide the dough into two halves with the metal cutter dipped in water. Again, the water will prevent the dough from sticking. Gently push the two halves apart, so they will not stick together, then let them rest on the work surface for approximately 5 minutes.

Place a baking stone in the center of the oven and a pan at the very bottom. Preheat the oven to 500°F.

Line two large peels with parchment paper sprinkled with coarse cornmeal.

Divide each half of the dough into three small loaves. Place three loaves on each peel while stretching them a little, remembering to leave a gap between them.

Ease the loaves onto the baking stone. Throw a cup of hot water into the hot pan at the bottom of the oven; then after 30 seconds mist the oven. Repeat this twice at 30-second intervals. Then lower the heat to 470°F. Bake the loaves for 20 to 25 minutes, depending on how you have chosen to shape them. When they are a beautifully golden color and deliciously crisp, they are done.

Badia a Coltibuono is one of Italy's many famous chef schools, as well as one of the most important houses for organic wines and olive oils. The estate has been owned by the same family since 1864, but it wasn't until 30 years ago that the lady of the house, Lorenza De'Medici, founded the chef school. Today the estate is run by her son, Guido Stucchi Prinetti. Through both him and Lorenza, I have been charmed and inspired by the simple, rustic, elegant, and appetizing Italian kitchen . . . also in terms of bread.

FOCACCIA AL COLTIBUONO

Equipment: baking pan approx. 10 x 14 inches

20 g fresh yeast
500 g sifted wheat flour
10 g fine salt
10 g (approx. 2 tsp) light cane sugar
50 g (approx. 2½ tbsp) high-quality olive oil, plus
a little extra for the pan and brushing the dough
Approx. 325 g lukewarm water

Decoration:
Needles from 3 to 5 fresh rosemary twigs
Flaked salt

Rub the yeast into the flour. Add the remaining ingredients, then mix and work the dough as shown in steps 2–4 on pages 48–49. Let it rest until doubled in volume.

Preheat the oven to 390°F.

Move the dough into a thoroughly oiled baking pan. Press and push to gently flatten it. Continue until the dough is approximately 1 inch high in an even layer in the pan. Let it proof for 15 minutes or more.

Brush the dough with the leftover olive oil; sprinkle on rosemary needles and salt flakes. Then gently press your fingertips several times into the dough to give it the "focaccia look." Bake for 20 to 25 minutes in the center of the oven until it is a light brown color.

The dough can also be divided into rolls and flattened to 0.4-inch-high mini pizzas topped with, for example, oven-dried cherry tomatoes, olives, pesto, potatoes, arugula leaves, cheese . . . whatever you feel like at the time.

Enjoying naan bread is a bit like enjoying pancakes: Everyone should be seated and ready, because the loaves are at their very best when served directly from the oven. That's what makes them second to none for light summer dinners on the terrace. In India naan is baked in very hot tandoori ovens. I bake mine on a baking stone in a burning hot oven. It takes 5 minutes and then the naan are ready for serving!

NAAN BREAD

Makes 8 naan

20 g fresh yeast
500 g sifted wheat flour
10 g salt
20 g (approx. 1 tbsp) neutral oil
50 g milk
2 large eggs
Approx. 200 g lukewarm water

For brushing:
Butter or plain yogurt

Rub the yeast into the flour, and add the remaining ingredients. Mix and work the dough as shown in steps 2–4 on pages 48-49, then let it rest until it has doubled in volume.

Preheat the convection oven, with baking stone, to 480 to 570°F—or as hot as possible.

When the dough is ready, degas it slightly, and divide it into eight pieces, then shape them into little balls. Roll out each ball to an oblong, 0.4-inch-thick loaf, and bake it immediately. Use a peel to place each loaf onto the burning-hot stone; you can bake two at a time. Each loaf is ready after 4 to 6 minutes.

Brush the hot loaf with butter or plain yogurt immediately before serving.

You can season your naan in many different ways: Brush them with butter, and sprinkle with, for example, finely chopped chili pepper or onion, ground coriander or cumin . . . any of your favorite flavors!

Serve the hot naan as soon as they're done, or wrap the loaves in a cloth to keep them warm until the whole batch is ready.

Crisp bread is, if anything, a Swedish national dish. It is claimed that in 85 percent of all Swedish kitchens you will find crisp bread ready for breakfast, lunch, or snack time. How much of it is actually home baked I have no idea, but I do know that even though almost all of our crisp bread is mass produced, it is not at all difficult to make it yourself. Give it a chance—home-baked crisp bread tastes magnificent!

CRISP BREAD

Makes 10 to 11 breads
Equipment: cookie cutter 1.5 to 2 inches across, spiked roller or fork

150 g whole-wheat flour
125 g whole-rye flour
125 g sifted rye flour
25 g fresh yeast
10 g salt
25 g (approx. 1 large tbsp) malt syrup
2 g (approx. 2 tsp) ground caraway seeds
50 g butter, room temperature
Approx. 250 g lukewarm water

Mix all the ingredients, then work the dough as shown in steps 2–4 on pages 48–49 until it is elastic but still rather sticky. Let it rest for 1 hour.

Preheat the convection oven to 480°F.

Dust the work surface thoroughly with flour. Turn the dough out onto the surface, and divide it into 75-g pieces. Shape them into balls, then roll out into flat discs, approximately 0.08 inches thick. Cut a hole in the middle of the discs using the cookie cutter. Prick the dough thoroughly with a fork or spiked roller.

Place the discs on sheet pans lined with parchment paper, and bake them for 6 minutes, until both the top sides and the bases have a beautiful light brown color.

Cool the crisp breads on a wire rack, and store them in an airtight cookie jar.

For everyone at Skærtoft Ester's apple strips—or "æblestænger"—speak of afternoon coffee and coziness. Ester is Jørgen's mother, and she ran the household at the farm for a generation before we took over. She is still very active and often spoils us with "a little something" for our coffee . . . she brings it along, freshly baked and temptingly fragrant, wrapped up in a cloth and lovingly transported in her braided basket. Ester has many delicious recipes in her little handwritten book. These apple strips are one of her best!

ESTER'S APPLE STRIPS

Makes 4 strips

40 g fresh yeast
600 g sifted wheat flour
5 g salt
50 g light cane sugar
2 large eggs
200 g butter
Approx. 200 g milk

Filling:
200 g butter
200 g light cane sugar
Thin slices of three sweet-tart apples
15 g white flour

For brushing and decoration:
1 egg, lightly beaten
Almond flakes and pearl sugar

Rub the yeast into the flour, and add the remaining ingredients. Mix and work the dough as shown in steps 2–4 on pages 48–49, until it is smooth and elastic.

Divide the dough into four pieces, and shape into balls. Cover with a cloth, and leave to rest on the table for 45 to 60 minutes. Roll each ball out into a 6 x 10-inch rectangle. Mix the butter and sugar, and spread it down the center of each rectangle. Turn the apple slices in some flour, and place in an even layer on the butter mix. Cover the filling up by folding the dough into the center from either side. Remember to seal both ends thoroughly. Place the strips on a sheet pan lined with parchment paper, and cover with a cloth. Let them proof for 45 minutes.

Preheat the oven to 430°F.

Brush the strips with egg, and decorate with almond flakes and pearl sugar.

Place the strips in the center of the oven, and bake for 20 to 25 minutes, until they turn a beautiful golden color.

TARTES AUX POMMES

Makes 16 to 18 tarts
Equipment: cookie cutter, 3 inches across

Our daughter, Marie-Louise, worked for Colette and Michel at the Boulangerie Ragot in Amboise for almost a year. As in all French bakeries, both baguettes and pains were baked and sold fresh several times a day, a tradition very different from that of most Danish bakeries. In addition to bread there were lots of lovely pastries for the sweet tooth. Tartes aux pommes was one of Marie-Louise's favorites. She never got the recipe, but we have been experimenting, and here is our very best version of how those beautiful tarts might be made.

175 g butter
250 g sifted spelt flour
20 g fresh yeast
20 g light cane sugar
50 g heavy cream

Filling:
250 g fine, sweet applesauce

For brushing and decoration:
1 egg, lightly beaten
25 g finely chopped almonds
30 g pearl sugar

Cube the cold butter, and rub it into the flour. Dissolve the yeast and sugar in the cream, and add it to the flour. Quickly mix the dough, and work it until it is smooth. Leave in a cool place for 30 minutes.

Preheat the oven to 430°F.

Roll the dough out on a floured work surface, and cut out 32 discs. Place half of the discs on a sheet pan lined with parchment paper. Place a spoonful of applesauce onto the center of each of these 16 discs. Brush all the edges thoroughly with egg, then place the remaining 16 discs on top of them. Firmly press all their edges together using a fork; then brush the little tartes aux pommes with egg, and decorate them with chopped almonds and pearl sugar.

The tarts should not proof but instead go straight into the oven and bake for 10 to 12 minutes.

Instead of applesauce, you can use mashed prunes or another sweet fruit compote—but then, of course, you can no longer call them "tartes aux pommes"!

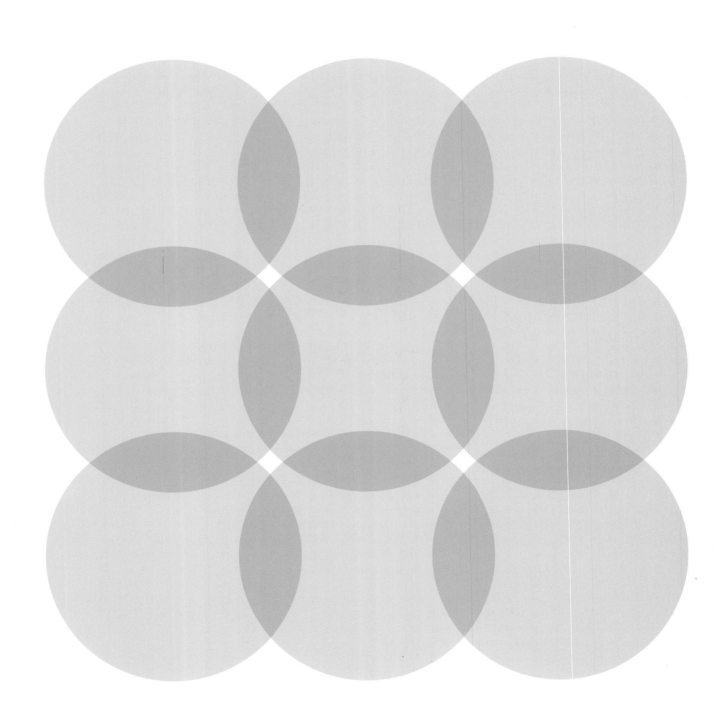

SOURDOUGHS AND STARTERS

SOURDOUGHS

In actual fact you do not need baker's yeast to bake bread. You only have to utilize the wild yeast that is all around us—in the air, on fresh fruit, in organic flour—to make a sourdough. You will then have the beginnings of a delicious, acidic bread, connecting you through a never-ending chain to bread bakers throughout the ages. Sourdough is probably the oldest way of fermenting bread. It is mentioned in many religious scriptures, including the Bible. Food historians believe that sourdough bread was already common in ancient Egypt and has therefore been eaten for over six thousand years.

Put simply, a sourdough consists of a mixture of flour and water. In some recipes a spoonful of honey, yogurt, grated apple, or mashed grapes is added, to more efficiently produce a reaction in the wild yeast. Yeast requires sugar and a warm and humid environment to develop. If you keep a bowl of flour and water at the appropriate temperature it will only be a few hours before the yeast spores and the Lactobacilli start to produce carbon dioxide and alcohol. It is characteristic for the slower-fermenting sourdough to develop a distinctively acidic taste and aroma and for the finished loaf to stay fresh longer.

The first time I tried to make a sourdough, I failed. Also the second and the third time—and that was the point at which I might have given up, writing off sourdough baking as an unobtainable skill. Luckily, I am stubborn, so it turned out to be "fourth time's the charm," perhaps because I started using two important tools—a whisk and a thermometer—along with a homemade trick that helps to give my sourdoughs the very best start in life. For me temperature is paramount when setting up a sourdough. In my experience the temperature of the sourdough in its initial phases needs to be around 82°F for a white sourdough and around 86°F for a rye sourdough. To get these numbers I use this formula: the desired temperature of the starter multiplied by 2, minus the temperature of the flour, equals the temperature the water should be when mixing the ingredients. For example, if the sourdough starter should be 82°F, and the flour is 66°F, then the water should be 98°F (i.e., 82° × 2 = 164° − 66° = 98°F). It's also been my experience that when mixing the flour and water it pays not just to mix them but to really beat the ingredients together thoroughly to get as much air into the starter as possible, and the fermentation process will start sooner and be more pronounced.

Finally—and this is very much a home-brewed technique for a good sourdough starter—I have figured out how to maintain that all-important temperature of 82°F by measuring the temperature of the mixing bowl and its contents at various locations around my kitchen. The ideal spot is on my kitchen radiator (set at room temperature) on a corkboard. That provides the perfect temperature . . . and my reward is a nicely bubbling sourdough with that lovely acidic fragrance.

My family laughs a bit at this arrangement . . . but they love the loaves that are the result!

As with your favorite potted plant, you can almost have a personal relationship with sourdough.

It can be fascinating and fulfilling to follow the day-to-day life of the sourdough, but it might also be a bit of a hassle if you're away for a longer period of time or are going on vacation. You might need to arrange for a friend or neighbor to look after your sourdough in addition to your plants. I've heard stories of sourdough nerds who have brought their sourdough with them on vacation, rather than risk its dying while they are away. I haven't gone quite that far yet—but I can totally understand it!

Sourdough is a symbiotic culture of Lactobacilli (*Lactobacillus* spp.) and wild yeast spores. It is used as a leaven for baking bread. Bread baked with sourdough has a special taste and aroma, which is mainly due to the lactic acid produced by the Lactobacilli.

The balance between the active microorganisms results in different types of sourdough. In earlier times, country housewives would be "assessed" according to how well they kept their sourdough. These days there are also much-coveted sourdoughs, including famous ones such as the San Francisco Sourdough. The local bakers claim that the naturally occurring yeast in their area is the best in the world. Don't imagine that such fine characteristics will easily travel, though, if you're planning on importing or exporting! A sourdough is a living thing and is of course influenced by any yeast spores present in the surrounding air. The San Francisco sourdough, for example, will be easily and willingly integrated into its new surroundings and will no longer be the original version. Similarly, I could set out to make a sourdough from an entirely original San Francisco recipe, but the end result would certainly be a product of Skærtoft.

Phytic acid, phytate, and phytase: Grain contains phytic acid, which precipitates salts called *phytate*. Large amounts of the iron, zinc, and magnesium found in flour and grain are bound with phytate, which means that these minerals are not available for immediate uptake by our bodies. However, a long fermentation period or the use of sourdough activates an enzyme, *phytase*, which breaks down phytate, thus releasing the iron, zinc, and magnesium in a usable form. This is one of the reasons that long-fermented bread and sourdough bread are healthier than ordinary bread.

WHITE SOURDOUGH STARTER

Equipment: 0.3-gallon (1-liter) container with airtight lid

Starter:
150 g stone-ground sifted wheat or spelt flour
50 g stone-ground whole-wheat or
whole-spelt flour
20 g honey
150 g water

Mix all the ingredients thoroughly in your container until the dough is soft but not liquid. Put a lid on the container, and place it in a warm place at 82°F for 36 to 48 hours. At that time the dough should show visible signs of fermentation and have a slight acidic smell.

First "feeding":
The starter (see above)
300 g stone-ground sifted wheat or spelt flour
150 g water

Mix all the ingredients thoroughly. Put the lid on the container, and keep it at 82°F. After 24 hours of fermentation, the starter should have a sweet-acidic aroma and show clear signs of fermentation. If not, then leave it until it shows clear signs of activity.

Second "feeding":
200 g dough from the first "feeding" batch
(discard the remainder)
400 g stone-ground strong white wheat
or spelt flour
200 g water

Mix the ingredients to a fairly compact dough. Shape it into a ball, and place it in the container. Put the lid on, and keep it at 82°F.

After approximately 12 hours you should be able to see clear signs of fermentation. To add more character to the starter, it should now be matured at a slower pace; therefore, leave it in the fridge for up to 48 hours.

The starter is now ready for its first use. Take 400 g of it for the bread you are going to bake. Add 700 to 800 g of stone-ground sifted wheat or spelt flour and 400 g water to the remainder of the starter. Mix thoroughly in the container, and shape into a ball. Close the container, and put it back in the fridge.

After 4 to 6 days, the starter is ready for use again. However, always remember to leave 400 g of dough remaining for the new starter, which should be fed (with 400 g water and 700 to 800 g of stone-ground sifted wheat or spelt flour) before going back in the fridge.

If you don't have the time to use the starter for baking, then you should do the following to ensure that it stays active and fresh:

400 g of the sourdough starter
(discard the remainder)
700 to 800 g stone-ground sifted wheat
or spelt flour
400 g water

Mix the ingredients thoroughly in the container, and shape the dough into a compact ball. Close the container, and place it in the fridge.

RYE SOURDOUGH STARTER

Equipment: 0.3-gallon (1-liter) container with airtight lid

Starter:
150 g water
150 g organic plain yogurt
200 g stone-ground whole-rye flour

Beat all the ingredients thoroughly in the container. Put a lid on the container, and keep in a warm place at 86°F for 24 hours.

"Feeding":
The starter (see above)
150 g water
200 g stone-ground whole-rye flour

Again, beat all the ingredients thoroughly in the container. Put a lid on the container, and keep in a warm place at 86°F for another 24 hours.

The sourdough, which should now be active and have a light and acidic aroma, is ready for use. When you have mixed the starter with your dough, remember to remove a portion (400 g) of the new dough to save for the next time you are going to bake. If you have only used a little of the starter, remember to "feed" it with 150 g water and 200 g stone-ground whole-rye flour before putting it back in the fridge, where it should stay between each bake or "feeding" from now on!

To slow the activity of the rye sourdough, you should, from now on, sprinkle the surface of the sourdough with a little salt before leaving it in the fridge.

Remember: Your sourdough should have a nice light and acidic aroma. If you look after it carefully, it will stay alive for years on end. The rule with sourdoughs is that "old is good"! In one of our baking classes, we welcomed the proud owner of a more than one-hundred-year-old sourdough. It has been "passed on through four generations, and lives a life in the hands of cousins, uncles and aunts." One might call it "a living antique" but with a lot more to it than just sentimental value!

When I am about to use my sourdough starter, I take it from the fridge and place it on the table to warm to the same temperature as the other ingredients that will be used in the new dough. A wheat sourdough starter needs a minimum of 2 hours. The rye starter I give at least 24 hours on the kitchen table, to wake it up and make sure that it is thriving with activity when it is added to the new dough.

Elin Værge, who was our closest neighbor for a couple of years, is a truly skilled bread baker. She does not go much for cakes and pastries but has a clear focus on healthy, coarse, delicious bread—and that includes rye bread. It was Elin who started me baking with rye sourdough . . . in fact, one of the sourdoughs I have in my fridge today was originally a present from Elin when we started up Skærtoft Mølle.

THE REAL RYE BREAD

Equipment: mixer, 1-gallon (3-liter) rye bread pan

Soaker:
200 g rye chops or pearl rye
Water
A pinch of salt

Dough:
The softened grains
400 g rye sourdough
20 g salt
50 g (approx. 2½ tbsp) barley malt syrup
350 g dark malt beer
450 g lukewarm water
800 g whole-rye flour

Decoration:
A little cracked rye

The night before, soak the rye chops or pearl rye in cold water with a pinch of salt. Leave the grains on the kitchen table overnight. Prior to using the grains, drain the excess water and give them a good shake.

Transfer the softened grains to the mixer, and add all other remaining ingredients. Mix for 10 minutes. The dough should have the consistency of a soft and sticky porridge and never be dry!

Take 400 g of the dough and place into an airtight container. Sprinkle a little salt onto the dough before you put the lid on, then put it into the fridge, for the next time you want to make rye bread. Place the rest of the dough in the rye bread pan, smooth its surface, and cover the tin with plastic wrap. If you prefer a distinctly acidic loaf, place the dough in the fridge for 24 hours, then remove the dough from the fridge, and leave at room temperature for a further 12 to 24 hours. If you prefer a less acidic loaf, just let the dough rest in the covered pan for 24 hours at room temperature. In both cases the rule is that the dough is oven ready when it almost reaches the top of the pan.

Preheat the oven to 320°F.

Splash a little water on the dough, and decorate with cracked rye if you wish. Place the pan on the second shelf up, and bake the bread for approximately 2½ hours. I recommend that you let the loaf cool for 24 hours before slicing it.

133

In supermarkets, as well as bakeries, it may be an almost impossible task to find rye bread made without wheat flour. The wheat "lifts" the heavy rye in terms of both flavor and volume. This is popular with many people—but not those suffering from wheat intolerance. This recipe caters both to the person trying to find a lighter rye bread and to the one who must say no to wheat.

SPELT RYE BREAD

Equipment: mixer, 1-gallon (3-liter) rye bread pan

Starter (day 1):
400 g rye sourdough
300 g water
350 g dark malt beer
20 g salt
50 g (approx. 2½ tbsp) barley malt syrup
300 g whole-spelt flour
300 g whole-rye flour
125 g seeds (linseeds, sunflower seeds, sesame seeds, or a mixture)

Dough (day 2):
All of the starter
400 g whole-rye flour
300 g water

Decoration:
Some of the seeds

Put all the ingredients into the mixing bowl, and mix for 10 minutes, then cover the dough, and leave it at room temperature until the next day.

Add flour and water to the starter. Mix again for 10 minutes using the mixer. The dough should have the consistency of a soft, sticky porridge. Take 400 g of the dough and place in an airtight container. Sprinkle a little salt onto it before you put the lid on. Then put it into the fridge, for the next time you want to make rye bread. Put the rest of the dough into the 1-gallon (3-liter) rye bread pan, and let it rest at room temperature for 6 hours, or until the dough almost reaches the top of the pan.

Preheat the oven to 355°F.

Prick the bread, splash a little water on the surface, and decorate with some seeds if you wish. Place the pan on the second shelf up, and bake for approximately 1½ hours.

If you can, wait until the next day before using the bread. When it has "settled" it is much easier to cut into slices. You can use paper muffin cups instead to bake delicious mini-loaves—great for the lunch box or as dinner rolls. The baking time for these is approximately 1 hour when placed in the center of the oven.

There are plenty of opportunities to experiment with flavor when you are baking rye bread. The relationship between flour, grains, seeds, and spices can be varied almost endlessly. For instance, I like to add a little fennel seed to the dough . . . but not everybody in the family likes that. This is why we always have different kinds of rye bread—so there's something for every taste. Having said that, I am pretty conservative when it comes to the liquids I use for my rye breads. Beer, water, and buttermilk—and I'm covered.

PUMPKIN SEED BREAD WITH BUTTERMILK

Equipment: mixer, 1-gallon (3-liter) rye bread pan

Dough:
400 g rye sourdough
625 g whole-rye flour
375 g whole-wheat flour
50 g cracked rye grains
125 g pumpkin seeds
Approx. 500 g buttermilk
Approx. 375 g water
25 g (approx. 1 tbsp) liquid honey
10 g malt flour
25 g salt

For brushing:
Melted butter

Decoration:
Pumpkin seeds

Blend all the ingredients, then mix with the mixer for 10 minutes. The dough should have the consistency of a soft and sticky porridge. Take 400 g of the dough and place it into an airtight container. Sprinkle a little salt onto it before putting the lid on, then place it into the fridge, for the next time you want to make rye bread. Scoop the rest of the dough into the 1-gallon (3-liter) rye bread pan. Let it rest at room temperature for 12 to 24 hours, or until the dough almost reaches the top of the pan.

Preheat the oven to 355°F.

Brush the loaf with a little melted butter. Decorate with pumpkin seeds, and bake it for approximately 1½ hours.

You can also use paper muffin cups, to bake delicious mini-loaves. Then the baking time is approximately 1 hour.

If you are looking for classic sourdough bread recipes, there is not much variation to be found. The recipe is strict: white sourdough, flour, water, and salt. As with a basic leavened dough, it is stripped right back to the essentials of bread. This is my version of the famous San Francisco Sourdough that I tasted in California. I have followed the instructions meticulously, but as the sourdough was made by me, this is really a Skærtoft copy of an American classic.

CLASSIC SOURDOUGH BREAD

Equipment: whisk, mixer, 12 x 18-inch loaf pan with high edges, 4.4-lb (2-kg) proofing basket

Starter:
300 g white sourdough
400 g sifted spelt or wheat flour
Approx. 500 g water

Dough:
All of the starter
Approx. 500 g sifted spelt or wheat flour
20 g salt

Starter: All ingredients must be at room temperature, approximately 70°F. Mix the sourdough, water, and flour, and beat it thoroughly, thereby adding as much air to the starter as possible. Leave the starter at 50 to 54°F overnight—in other words, not in the fridge!

Dough: Scrape the dough into the mixer bowl. Add the flour, and set the mixer to run for 5 minutes. Then add the salt, and continue the mixing until the dough is satiny and very elastic but also very soft. Scrape the dough into the oiled loaf pan. Dust a little flour on top, and allow to rest for 1 hour.

Lift the dough out onto a floured work surface, gently push it to make a square, fold it in half, turn it through 90°, then stretch it and fold it into thirds. Place the dough in the pan, and let it rest for another hour. Repeat this process twice. It is important to really stretch the dough. You will feel quite clearly that its strength and elasticity improve with each round of folding.

After the final resting period, turn the dough out onto a floured work surface. Shape into a tight loaf, place in a floured proofing basket—top side down—and let it proof until it's nearly doubled in volume, 3 to 4 hours.

Preheat the oven, with baking stone, to 480°F.

Transfer the loaf onto a dusted peel. Score the dough in a check pattern. Generously mist the oven, then load the bread into the hot oven. After 10 minutes, lower the heat to 390°F, and bake for 30 to 45 minutes more.

The seeds and the malt flour in this recipe speak so warmly to the acidity of the sourdough that this bread has become one of our absolute favorites . . . and also a favorite of the visitors who have been served it. When making the seed mix, I always add some fennel seeds, unless I'm able to replace them with a handful of seeds from my sweet cicely plant, also known as Spanish chervil. It has the same aniseed taste as fennel but with a softer tone that I greatly enjoy. However, I can only harvest its seeds in small amounts; the fennel seeds, fortunately, I can buy all year round.

SOURDOUGH BREAD WITH SEEDS AND MALT FLOUR

Equipment: 2.2-lb (1-kg) proofing basket

Dough:
450 g sifted spelt flour
50 g malt flour
10 g fresh yeast
10 g salt
50 g white sourdough
50 g mixed seeds
Approx. 350 g lukewarm water

Seed mix:
15 g of each of the following:
Linseeds, sesame seeds, pumpkin seeds, dark poppy seeds, sunflower seeds, and fennel seeds

Decoration:
Leftover seed mix

Mix the ingredients, and work the dough thoroughly, as shown in steps 2–4 on pages 48–49. Shape the dough into a ball, and place it in a lightly floured bowl, then leave it to rest until it's doubled in volume.

Turn the dough onto a floured work surface, and degas slightly. Shape into a ball, and place back in the bowl. Let it rest for 1 to 3 hours, or until it's doubled in volume.

Turn the dough out onto a floured work surface. Degas slightly, shape into a round loaf, and place, top side down, in a floured proofing basket. Cover and proof for approximately 45 minutes, or until nearly doubled in volume.

Preheat the convection oven, with baking stone, to 480°F.

Ease the loaf onto a peel that has been lightly dusted with coarse cornmeal. Score the loaf; then, using a spray bottle, generously mist the inside of the oven with water. Ease the loaf from the peel onto the baking stone. Spray more water into the oven. After 5 minutes, lower the heat to 390°F, and bake the loaf for 20 to 35 minutes more.

The pear season at Skærtoft begins with the Count Moltke variety and ends with Conference. The Count, who ripens in early September, never makes it farther than the fruit bowl before he's eaten. Conference pears are not perfect until a month later. They look like little green pixie hats, and if the spring has been warm and frost free, then the branches will be weighed down with fruit. When Conference is ripe, this juicy, sweetly aromatic pear can be used for almost anything—including bread.

PEAR AND SOURDOUGH BREAD

Equipment: mixer

Dough:
125 g white sourdough
200 g sifted spelt or wheat flour
150 g durum wheat flour plus 50 g for toasting
5 g fresh yeast
70 g sour cream or yogurt
10 g salt
100 g firm ripe pears, peeled and finely cubed
Sunflower oil to brush the bowl
Approx. 100 g water

For brushing:
Egg white, beaten with a little cold water

Take the sourdough out of the fridge at least 1 hour before using. Work in the yeast, water, and 100 g of the wheat/spelt flour. Let it rest in a warm place for 1 hour.

Toast the 50 g durum flour in a dry frying pan at low heat for approximately 5 minutes, until golden. Allow to cool.

Mix the durum flour, both toasted and regular, with the remaining 100 g wheat/spelt flour. Add the sourdough mix along with all the remaining ingredients. Mix the dough for 10 minutes using your mixer, shape it into a ball, and place it in an oiled bowl. Let it rest for 2 to 3 hours until it has doubled in volume.

Turn the dough out onto a floured work surface, and degas slightly. Shape the dough into a tight ball, place it onto a peel lined with parchment paper, and let it proof until it has nearly doubled in volume.

Preheat the oven, with baking stone, to 480°F.

Brush the loaf with the beaten egg white, then score it. Generously mist the oven with water from a spray bottle, then ease the loaf and the parchment paper onto the baking stone. Spray with water again, repeating twice at 30-second intervals. Then lower the heat to 390°F, and bake the bread for 30 to 35 minutes more.

PÂTE FERMENTÉE, POOLISH, AND BIGA

All starters have this in common: Unlike sourdoughs, which will last forever, starters have only a limited shelf life. They are, however, extremely easy to work with, add lots of extra flavor, and make healthier bread, so the effort of working with them does pay off—very handsomely! In this book I use the common designation "starter" for all types of starters used in my recipes. Here is a list, however, of some of the most classic examples of starters.

Pâte fermentée: French for "old dough," it consists of flour, water, salt, and yeast and is the only starter containing salt. In its simplest form it could be just a piece of dough from your latest bake, but it may also be freshly made, mixed the night before you use it. A pâte fermentée heightens the flavor in the finished loaf.

Poolish is a mix of equal measures water and flour and a tiny bit of yeast, 1 to 2 percent of the total quantity of flour. Once it has been mixed, the poolish should resemble pancake dough. It contains no salt. A mature poolish has a sweet-acidic nutty aroma and feels almost like silk to the touch. It increases your dough's ability to stretch, which results in a more voluminous loaf. The tradition for baking with a poolish was brought to Paris by Polish bakers. From there the technique has spread to the rest of the world.

Biga is the Italian word for starter. A biga may either be like compact dough or soft like the poolish. There is no salt in a biga, only flour, water, and yeast. The amount of yeast is like that of the poolish—.1 to .2 percent of the total flour quantity.

Soaking or softening of grains increases the flavor of the grains and softens them to prevent them from ruining the gluten structure when you make your dough. It also prevents you from cracking your teeth when eating loaves with whole grains in them. As opposed to dry grains, the soaked grains do not "steal" any moisture from the dough during its resting time.

Soak the grains in cold water, or if they are particularly hard, pour some boiling water on them. In both cases water and grains should be mixed thoroughly, and the bowl then covered with plastic wrap or a lid. If the grains have high enzymatic activity—as is the case with rye—adding a little salt to the mixture may lower the enzymatic activity.

Autolyse is another kind of "soaking" and is a term known from natural sciences. It refers to a period of rest after the initial mixing of flour and water, before the addition of yeast and other ingredients. The autolyse kick-starts the dough, thereby making it develop more quickly than usual. It allows for better absorption of water and helps the gluten and starches align. Breads made with autolysed dough are easier to shape and have more volume and improved structure. This method was "invented" by the French professor Raymond Calvel.

Scalding is an old Nordic method for softening the coarse whole-grain flour, and thus making it easier to work with. An additional bonus is that the finished loaves taste better and stay fresher longer (see, for instance, the following recipe for Elin's Walnut Bread). The method has experienced renewed interest because of the growing interest in Nordic cooking and baking traditions.

We have a huge old walnut tree in the garden. It bears an incredible amount of fruit, which we pick every August to make Walnut Aquavit. Later in the year we use the ripe nuts when they are fresh, or, as in this recipe, dried and baked into bread. We gather the nuts in tight competition with the crows, which fly nonstop around the garden between the tree and their hideaways. They literally pluck the nuts from the branches, especially the topmost ones, where we don't stand a chance. This walnut bread is a Skærtoft classic, first baked by our neighbor Elin Værge.

ELIN'S WALNUT BREAD

Makes 2 loaves

Scalding:
75 g whole-spelt flour
100 g finely chopped walnuts
Approx. 250 g boiling water

Dough:
10 g fresh yeast
675 g sifted spelt flour
200 g plain yogurt
15 g (approx. ¾ tbsp) walnut oil
15 g salt
25 g (approx. 1¼ tbsp) barley malt syrup
Approx. 80 g water
The scalded flour mix

For brushing:
One egg, beaten with a little water

Mix the whole-spelt flour, chopped walnuts, and boiling water thoroughly, and allow to soak for about 1 hour.

Rub the yeast into the flour. Add this along with the remaining ingredients to the whole-grain/walnut mix, then mix and work the dough as shown in steps 2–4 on pages 48–49. Rest the dough in the fridge overnight.

Take the dough from the fridge, turn it out onto a floured work surface, divide it into two equal-size pieces, and shape them into tight freestanding loaves. You may also divide each piece into two or three strands, then either twist or braid them into beautiful loaves. Place onto a sheet pan covered with parchment paper, then leave them to proof in a warm place until they have nearly doubled in volume.

Preheat the oven to 430°F.

Brush the loaves with the beaten egg, and place them on the second shelf up. After 10 minutes, lower the heat to 390°F, and bake for 30 to 40 minutes more.

The terms "landbrød," "pain de campagne," or "farm bread" cover many different recipes from many different countries. What they have in common is that they arose to serve a way of life in which solid, nourishing food was essential and would enable farmers to meet the hard, physical demands of working the land. As luck would have it, this type of bread also tastes fantastic; the dough and the softened grains work together beautifully, enhancing both the flavor and the nutritional value.

FARM BREAD WITH CRACKED WHEAT

Makes 2 loaves
Equipment: proofing baskets or loaf pans, mixer

Starter:
5 g fresh yeast
200 g water
120 g sifted wheat flour
Mix and leave at room temperature for
12 hours, or overnight.

Soaker:
Boiling water
100 g cracked wheat grains
Parboil the grains, then leave to soak in
the water for 12 hours, or overnight.

Dough:
The starter
The soaked wheat grains, well drained
Approx. 300 g lukewarm water
100 g plain yogurt
150 g tart, grated apples
20 g salt
200 g whole-wheat flour
700 g sifted wheat flour

Mix the ingredients, then finish the dough in the mixer. It should be thoroughly mixed and still very soft.

Leave it to rest for approximately 3 hours, or until doubled in volume. Divide it, then shape into two oblong loaves. Leave to proof until nearly doubled in volume, in floured proofing baskets or in greased loaf pans.

Preheat oven to 390°F.

Brush the loaves with some cold coffee, then sprinkle on a little extra cracked wheat. Bake on the bottom shelf of the oven for 30 to 45 minutes.

The ceramist Sigrid Hovmand makes and sells her pottery on the island of Samsø. Together with chef Søren Ørum, from the restaurant "By the Pond," she has created an extraordinarily beautiful and quite unique "loaf pan" of unglazed stoneware. It's a distinguished example of how aesthetic handicraft in the kitchen can go hand in hand with everyday use. I am a great fan of Sigrid's cocottes. They bake beautiful bread with a lovely moist crumb and a crunchy crust. My first cocotte bread was my own recipe, with ramsons. This recipe is one of Sigrid's, which I have adjusted to the way we make our dough.

STONE COCOTTE SAMSØ BREAD

Equipment: stoneware cocotte for 2.2 lb (1 kg) of dough

Starter:
90 g whole-rye flour
200 g boiling water
Mix together, and allow to cool. Leave out overnight in a container with a lid.

Dough:
15 g fresh yeast
500 g sifted wheat flour
All of the starter
15 g salt
Approx. 225 g lukewarm water

Decoration:
Whole-rye flour

Rub the yeast into the flour. Mix the starter and the salt, then add this to the flour along with the water. Mix and work the dough as shown in steps 2–4 on pages 48–49. The dough must be a bit stickier than normal yeast-fermented dough. Let it rest for 1½ hours.

Lightly oil both the base and lid of the cocotte.

Gently turn the dough out onto a floured work surface, shape it into a tight round loaf, and place it in the cocotte. Press and push with your hands to make sure the dough reaches the edges of the cocotte. You may moisten your hands with water to prevent the dough from sticking. Let the loaf proof for approximately 1 hour.

Sprinkle the surface of the dough with whole-rye flour, then score the loaf. Put the lid on the cocotte, and place it on a sheet pan on the second shelf up in a COLD oven. Set the temperature to 390°F. (I do not recommend using a convection oven for this recipe as it will ruin the cocotte.) After 1¼ hours the bread is finished. Remove from the cocotte immediately, and allow to cool on a wire rack.

Important: Every time the cocotte is used, it picks up a light coating of oil. Wipe it after use with a damp cloth, or rinse it with hot water—no soap!

"With Skærtoft Mill's whole-wheat flour you get more vitamins and minerals in the finished loaf. During a long resting period (up to 24 hours) the flour makes for really stable dough. It gives you bread with a lovely dense crumb and a nice crust, and plenty to chew on. The loaf has a wonderful fragrance. Its flavor is 'truly wheaty', with a hint of nuts."

The above is a quote from the jury when our whole-wheat flour was awarded the Danish Organic Gold Medal in 2006. That day we toasted with the prize-winning, champagne-worthy Fejø Cider. Once we were home, the medals inspired us to make this bread, which we treasure and call our Gold Medal Bread.

GOLD MEDAL BREAD

Starter:
125 g whole-wheat flour
5 g fresh yeast
Approx. 90 g water

Dough:
200 g whole-wheat flour
300 g sifted wheat flour
10 g fresh yeast
All of the starter
10 g salt
250 g hard apple cider
Approx. 90 g water

Mix and whip the ingredients for the starter thoroughly, and leave it in the fridge for 12 to 24 hours.

Remove it from the fridge 1 hour before using.

Mix the two types of flour thoroughly, rub in the yeast, then rub in the starter. Add the remaining ingredients, and work the dough as shown in steps 2-4 on pages 48-49. Let the dough rest in a warm place for 1 hour.

Turn the dough out onto a floured work surface, and degas slightly. Then shape it into a ball, and leave it to rest until it has doubled in volume.

Preheat the convection oven, with baking stone, to 480°F.

Turn the dough out onto a floured work surface. Shape it into a round, tight loaf; place it onto a floured couche; cover it; and let it proof until it has nearly doubled in volume.

Transfer the bread onto a peel lightly dusted with coarse cornmeal. Sprinkle a little whole-grain flour on the loaf, and score it. Generously mist the inside of the oven with water, and ease the loaf onto the baking stone. Spray more water into the oven, and repeat twice at 30-second intervals. Lower the heat after 7 to 8 minutes to 410°F. Bake the bread for approximately 25 to 30 minutes more.

CELEBRATION BUNS

Makes 14 to 17 buns

For many, many years these South Jutland Birthday Buns have been an essential at children's birthday parties. I usually have some ready in the freezer, just in case of unexpected visitors. I know the recipe by heart, and it wasn't until I visited the Bertinet Kitchen in England that the original Birthday Buns experienced competition from the excellent Bath Buns. Now I have taken the best elements of both and combined them, in this delicious new version of our local treat.

Starter:
5 g fresh yeast
125 g sifted spelt or wheat flour
Approx. 125 g water

Dough:
15 g fresh yeast
400 g sifted spelt or wheat flour
All of the starter
5 g (approx. ¼ tsp) salt
125 g softened butter
50 g cane sugar
2 large eggs
150 g whole milk
2 tsp ground cardamom (can be left out, but then they're no longer genuine South Jutland Birthday Buns!)

For brushing:
Traditional: one egg, beaten with a little water, OR
English glaze: 75 g light cane sugar mixed with 150 g whole milk

Starter: Rub the yeast into the flour, add the water, then beat until the starter becomes even and smooth. Cover it, and leave in the fridge overnight. If baking the buns on the same day, let the covered starter rest at room temperature for 2 to 3 hours.

Dough: Rub the yeast into the flour, add the remaining ingredients, then mix and work the dough as shown in steps 2–4 on pages 48–49. Let it rest for 1 hour. Turn the dough out onto a floured work surface, degas slightly, then let it rest in the bowl until it has doubled in volume.

Turn the dough out onto a floured work surface, make it into a long sausage shape, and divide into 60-g pieces. Roll them into small buns, and place them on a sheet pan lined with parchment paper. Cover the buns, and let them proof until they have nearly doubled in volume.

Preheat the oven to 390°F.

According to Southern Danish tradition, the party buns should be brushed with beaten eggs mixed with a little water before going into the oven. But you can also use the "English glazing": heat the sugar and milk until the sugar has melted. Let it cool, then glaze the buns before baking.

Place the buns in the center of the oven, and bake them for 15 to 20 minutes, until they become a light golden color.

Remove the buns from the oven.

If you have used the glazing, you should glaze the buns a second time while they are still warm from the oven.

157

The starter for this heart-shaped bread is a textbook pâte fermentée. The bread is also an example of my love of baking bread in cocottes. The cocottes are not necessarily made from clay or stone; here I have used a heart-shaped pie dish from Le Creuset, made from cast iron. The result, as you can see, is the crustiest of crusts, cracked in delicate patterns from where the bread came out of the hot cocotte and began to cool.

HEART-SHAPED BREAD

Equipment: 2.8-lb (1½-liter) heart-shaped cocotte (or other shape)

Starter:
3 g fresh yeast
150 g sifted wheat flour
5 g salt
120 g lukewarm water

Dough:
5 g fresh yeast
All of the starter
240 g sifted wheat flour
5 g salt
Approx. 150 g water

Starter: Rub the yeast into the flour, and add remaining ingredients.

Mix the dough thoroughly, without working it. Shape it into a ball, and place it in an oiled bowl. Let it proof until doubled in volume.

Turn the dough out onto a floured work surface. Degas slightly, and shape it into a ball. Put it back in the bowl, and let it rest in the fridge overnight.

Dough: Take the starter from the fridge 1 to 2 hours before using.

Rub the yeast and then the starter into the flour, and add the remaining ingredients. Mix and work the dough as shown in steps 2-4 on pages 48–49, then let it rest for 2 hours.

Turn the dough out onto a floured work surface, degas slightly, fold and shape it into a ball, then place it into the bowl to rest for another 2 hours.

Turn the dough out onto a floured work surface, and degas slightly. Fold and shape the dough into a tight ball and place it in the heart-shaped dish. Make sure to oil both the bottom and lid of the dish before placing in the loaf. Let it settle for 5 minutes, before gently pressing it with damp hands until it fills out the dish. Cover the loaf, and let it proof until nearly doubled in volume.

Put the lid on the dish, and place in a cold oven. Set the oven to 390°F. Baking time is approximately 1½ hours. Remove from the dish immediately, and cool on a wire rack.

The nutty aroma of this poolish is enhanced by the spelt flour. Not only does the poolish add a fantastic flavor to the dough, it also makes it silky soft and appealing to the touch. The finished loaf just smells, tastes, and looks so good . . . the adjectives start queuing up whenever I try to describe it. You couldn't ask for better rewards from the modest effort it takes to make bread!

SPELT-DURUM BREAD

Makes 2 to 3 loaves

Starter:
2 g fresh yeast
300 g lukewarm water
300 g sifted spelt flour

Dough:
8 g fresh yeast
300 g sifted spelt flour
100 g whole-spelt flour
200 g durum wheat flour
All of the starter
20 g salt
Approx. 300 g lukewarm water

Starter: Dissolve the yeast in the water, add the flour, then whip until the starter is soft and supple. Let it rest at room temperature for 12 to 16 hours, or overnight.

Dough: Rub the yeast into the flour. Add the remaining ingredients, then mix and work the dough as described previously. It should be very soft and elastic. Fold it several times, and shape it into a ball. Let it rest for 1 hour. Then turn the dough out onto a floured work surface, degas slightly, and fold and shape into a ball again. Let it rest for another hour.

Turn the dough out onto a floured work surface, and divide it into two or three equal pieces, depending on the desired loaf size. Fold the pieces of dough lightly without degassing them. Dust them, and let them rest on the work surface for 30 minutes, loosely covered with a cloth. Then shape the dough into oblong loaves. Place them on a floured couche, pulling up folds of linen so that the loaves do not stick together during proofing. Cover with a cloth, and leave to proof for 1 to 1½ hours, or until nearly doubled in volume.

Preheat the convection oven, with baking stone, to 480°F.

Transfer the loaves to peels that have been lightly dusted with coarse cornmeal. Generously mist the oven with water using a spray bottle, ease the loaves onto the baking stone, and spray some more water into the oven. Repeat twice more at 30-second intervals. Bake the loaves for 20 to 25 minutes depending on size.

Professional bakers developed the biga in Italy when yeast, by being quicker and easier to work with, defeated sourdough, which until then had been the only leaven used for thousands of years. The Italians had to acknowledge, however, that yeast alone could not deliver the excellent flavor and texture so characteristic of sourdough bread. The biga was the solution to that problem. In a classic biga the ratio of water to flour is 60/100. This gives you a solid starter, which develops a light, nutty flavor when left to ferment for 12 to 16 hours. There are recipes for soft bigas with a 50/50 ratio of flour to water—which would be known in France as a poolish!

RAISIN-WALNUT BREAD

Makes 2 loaves

Starter:
115 g sifted wheat flour
115 g whole-wheat flour
3 g fresh yeast
140 g water

Dough:
620 g sifted wheat flour
70 g whole-wheat flour
7 g fresh yeast
All of the starter
15 g salt
25 g (approx. 1 large tbsp) liquid honey
150 g chopped walnuts
150 g golden raisins
Approx. 500 g lukewarm water

Mix the starter ingredients thoroughly. Shape this rather compact dough into a ball, then leave it to rest in the fridge overnight.

Turn the starter out onto a floured work surface and cut into smaller pieces; let them rest for 1 hour under a cover.

Mix the two types of flour thoroughly. Rub in the yeast and the starter, then add the remaining ingredients. Mix and work the dough as shown in steps 2–4 on pages 48–49. Let the dough rest for 1 hour, then turn it out onto a floured work surface, degas slightly, shape into a ball, and leave to rest for another hour.

Turn the dough out onto a floured work surface, degas slightly, divide it in half, and shape into two loaves. Let them proof on a floured couche until they have nearly doubled in volume.

Preheat the convection oven, with baking stone, to 480°F.

Transfer the loaves to peels that have been lightly dusted with coarse cornmeal. Score the loaves. Generously mist the oven, ease the loaves onto the baking stone, then spray more water into the oven. Spray again after 30 seconds, then lower the heat to 390°F. Bake the loaves for 20 to 25 minutes, depending on their size.

163

ROSEMARY BREAD

Makes 2 to 3 loaves

Starter:
5 g fresh yeast
320 g sifted wheat flour
225 g water

Dough:
All of the starter
400 g sifted wheat flour
10 g salt
¼ tsp freshly ground pepper
8 g fresh yeast
170 g cold mashed potatoes
15 g olive oil
10 g (approx. 3½ tbsp) fresh, chopped rosemary
50 g chopped garlic cloves, roasted in some oil
Approx. 225 g lukewarm water

Decoration:
Coarse cornmeal for sprinkling
Olive oil

Starter: Rub the yeast into the flour, add the water, and mix the starter ingredients thoroughly. Then work the dough as shown in steps 2-4 on pages 48-49. Shape it into a ball, and place it in an oiled bowl, making sure all of the surface is covered in oil. Leave the dough to rest for 2 to 4 hours or until it has doubled in volume.

Turn the starter out onto a floured work surface, degas slightly, then fold and shape into a ball. Put it back in the bowl, and let it rest in the fridge for 12 hours, or overnight.

Take the starter from the fridge 1 hour prior to using it. Place it on a floured work surface, and cut it into smaller pieces. Leave these to rest for 1 hour under a cover.

Dough: Sift the flour, salt and black pepper into a bowl. Rub in the starter, then add the mashed potatoes, oil, rosemary, and water. Mix and work the dough as described previously. Once the dough is ready, shape and flatten it into a square. Spread the roasted garlic cloves onto the dough, then fold the edges across, covering the cloves. Shape the dough into a ball, and place it in an oiled bowl. Give it a couple of turns to make sure that all of the surface is covered in oil. Let it rest until doubled in volume.

Preheat the oven to 410°F.

Turn the dough out onto a floured work surface, degas slightly, divide in half, and shape each half into a tight round loaf. Place these a distance apart on a sheet pan lined with parchment paper. Let them proof until nearly doubled in volume.

Brush the loaves lightly with olive oil, score them, then place them in the center of the oven. You can sprinkle some cornmeal on top, for decoration. The baking time is 40 to 45 minutes.

Rosemary means something like "the dew of the sea." Wild rosemary thrives along the Mediterranean, and it is said that in olden days the sailors could recognize the Spanish and Arabic coastlines from the scent of rosemary alone. The herb is said to strengthen memory, have antibacterial properties, and have a positive effect on headaches, blood circulation, rheumatism, and stress. It symbolizes faithfulness and also keeps evil spirits at bay. And it tastes great: one more very good reason to use rosemary in bread.

Ciabatta, "the slipper bread," came from Liguria but spread from there to the whole of Italy, with small but significant variations along the way … significant to connoisseurs, at least. The loaf went on to conquer the rest of the world. Using whole-grain flour will give you ciabatta integrale, while using milk will result in ciabatta al latte. There are variations involving olive oil and spices, and then there are also the little slippers that are used for the toasted sandwiches called panini, or panino, if there's only one! The slipper is here to stay, and who would want to be without it?

CIABATTA

Makes 3 loaves

Starter:
3 g fresh yeast
320 g sifted spelt flour
340 g water

Dough:
10 g fresh yeast
400 g sifted spelt flour
All of the starter
15 g salt
Approx. 170 g water

Rub the yeast into the flour, add the water, and mix thoroughly into a thick starter. Rest it in the fridge overnight.

Remove the starter from the fridge at least 1 hour before using. Rub the yeast into the flour, then add the starter and the remaining ingredients. Mix and work the dough as shown in steps 2–4 on pages 48–49. The dough should stay quite soft. Shape it into a ball, and place it in an oiled bowl. Give it a couple of turns to make sure all of the dough is covered in oil. Let it rest for 30 minutes.

Turn the dough out onto a floured work surface. Stretch it gently, folding it without squashing it. Repeat this a couple of times, before shaping the dough into a ball and putting it back in the oiled bowl. Let it rest until it has nearly doubled in volume.

Preheat the convection oven, with baking stone, to 500°F.

Thoroughly flour your baker's linen. Turn the dough out onto a well-floured work surface. Do not degas the dough, but very gently cut it into three equal pieces. Stretch each piece to form a rectangle, then fold to form another rectangle of 4 x 6 inches. Place the folded loaf onto the floured baker's linen. Repeat with the remaining two pieces of dough. Remember to pull up folds between each loaf to prevent them from sticking during proofing. You may spray the top side with a little oil. Cover the loaves, and let them proof until they have nearly doubled in volume.

Transfer the loaves from the baker's linen to peels dusted with coarse cornmeal. If there isn't enough room for all three loaves, bake them separately. Generously mist the oven with water from a spray bottle. Ease the loaves onto the baking stone. Spray more water into the oven, then repeat twice at 30-second intervals. Lower the heat to 430°F, and bake the ciabatta for 20 to 30 minutes.

Half an ounce of malt flour in a dough can add a surprising new character to the bread, a more intense flavor, a deeper color, and a sweet, delicate aroma redolent of beer. I have emphasized this latter quality further by using beer and malt syrup in the end dough. The three ingredients of malt flour, malt syrup, and beer come from the same source—that is, germinated grains, in this case barley—and they suit each other very well in this dark, tasty, beautiful bread.

MALT FLOUR BREAD

Starter:
220 g sifted wheat flour
5 g fresh yeast
150 g water

Dough:
10 g fresh yeast
325 g sifted wheat flour
10 g salt
25 g (approx. 1 large tbsp) malt syrup
20 g malt flour
All of the starter
15 g (approx. 1½ tbsp) olive oil
Approx. 225 g wheat beer

For brushing:
Egg whites beaten with a little water

Thoroughly mix the ingredients for the starter. Shape the dough into a ball. Let it rest in the fridge overnight.

Remove the starter from the fridge at least 1 hour before using it.

Rub the yeast into the flour, add the salt, malt syrup, and malt flour, and mix thoroughly. Rub in the starter, then add the oil and beer. Mix and work the dough as shown in steps 2-4 on pages 48-49. Shape it into a ball, and place in an oiled bowl, giving it a couple of turns to make sure the surface is covered in oil. Leave the dough to rest until it has nearly doubled in volume.

Turn the dough out onto a floured work surface. Do not degas the dough, but fold it gently instead, and shape it into an oblong loaf. Line a sheet pan with parchment paper dusted with coarse cornmeal, and place the loaf onto it. Proof until nearly doubled in volume.

Preheat the oven to 480°F.

Brush the loaf, and score it. Generously mist the inside of the oven, and place the loaf on the second shelf up. Spray more water into the oven, and repeat twice at 30-second intervals. Then lower the heat to 410°F, and bake the bread for 40 to 45 minutes. The bread will get very dark because of the malt flour.

The nutty flavor of spelt combined with the sweetness of barley is the perfect combination for a modern version of the classic sifted wheat and rye flour. I've mixed spelt and barley in a ratio of 70/30, because this blend gives me the best balance of flavor and at the same time a dough that rises beautifully in spite of the barley, which, like rye, contains very little gluten.

SPELT AND BARLEY BREAD

Equipment: 2.2-lb (1-kg) proofing basket

Starter:
300 g sifted barley flour
400 g sifted spelt flour
20 g fresh yeast
700 g cold water

Dough:
All of the starter
300 g sifted spelt flour
20 g salt

Mix the two types of flour for the starter. Rub in the yeast, then add water. Mix the dough and let it rest in the fridge overnight.

Let the starter warm for at least 1 hour. Then add the flour and salt, and mix and work the dough as shown in steps 2-4 on pages 48-49. It's important to add air to the dough and that the finished dough is tight and elastic but also relatively soft.

Dust your work surface, and fold and shape the dough into a ball. Let it rest in the bowl until it's doubled in volume.

Turn the dough out onto a floured work surface. Degas slightly, and shape it into a round loaf. Place it top side down in a proofing basket, and let it proof until it has nearly doubled in volume.

Preheat the convection oven, with baking stone, to 480°F.

Turn the dough out onto a dusted peel. Score the loaf. Mist the inside of the oven, ease the loaf onto the baking stone, then mist in the oven again. Repeat after 30 seconds. After 5 minutes of baking, lower the heat to 430°F, and bake the bread for 30 to 40 minutes more.

173

Before starting up Skærtoft Mølle, we visited many smaller mills around Europe. One of them was Saltå Kvarn in Sweden, a fascinating company, where attitude is turned into action with a blooming milling enterprise, a large bakery, a cozy café, and a little store selling all the goodies from the mill. Saltå Kvarn is biodynamic, and within the bakery each and every dough is worked by hand. There are no compromises, and their motto is: "The efforts of the farmer, miller, and baker should all be felt in the mouth!" My Swedish baguettes are inspired by the ones from Saltå Kvarn.

SWEDISH BAGUETTES

Makes 3 loaves

Starter:
100 g whole-spelt flour
200 g sifted spelt flour
5 g fresh yeast
300 g water

Dough:
200 g durum flour
200 g sifted spelt flour
50 g malt flour
All of the starter
25 g (approx. 1 large tbsp) honey
Approx. 200 g water
15 g salt

Mix and whip the ingredients for the starter dough, then leave it at 50 to 53°F for 12 hours or overnight.

Mix the durum flour, spelt flour, and malt flour. Add the starter, honey, and water, then mix and work the dough as described previously. When it is half finished, add the salt, then finish the dough. Shape into a ball, and let it rest until doubled in volume.

Cut the dough into three equal pieces, and shape them into baguettes. Let them proof on a floured couche. Pull up a fold between each baguette to prevent them from sticking to each other while proofing. Cover them and leave to proof until they have nearly doubled in volume.

Preheat the convection oven, with baking stone, to 480°F.

Transfer the baguettes onto peels dusted with coarse cornmeal. Score them, then mist the inside of the oven with water. Ease the baguettes onto the baking stone, and spray more water into the oven. Repeat after 1 minute. Lower the heat to 390°F, and bake the baguettes for 16 to 22 minutes.

I have two inspiring books written by chef Heston Blumenthal, from The Fat Duck *restaurant in England:* In Search of Perfection, *volumes I and II. They can be read as essays about food, cultural history, and travel— and also, of course, as cookbooks. Their common theme is the search to find the most outstanding examples of recipes for what we would otherwise call "junk food"—the pizzas, burgers, and "fish 'n' chips," for example, which are devoured by millions of people worldwide every minute. Heston Blumenthal manages the sublime. I have adjusted his "ultimate burger bun" recipe to a more down-to-earth Skærtoft version—and it has been reviewed with glowing stars by everyone.*

BURGER BUNS

Makes 10 to 11 buns
Equipment: Mixer

Starter:
5 g fresh yeast
200 g sifted spelt flour
200 g cold water

Dough:
All of the starter
100 g egg yolks
35 g (approx. 3 tbsp) low-fat milk
200 g sifted spelt flour
50 g light cane sugar
10 g fine salt
10 g fresh yeast
50 g softened butter
20 g (approx. 1 large tbsp) neutral oil

For brushing:
1 egg plus 1 egg yolk
5 g (approx. 1 tsp) water
3 g (approx. ½ tsp) salt

Decoration:
Sesame seeds

Starter: Rub the yeast into the flour, add the water, and mix everything thoroughly. Pour the dough into a container at least four times the volume of the mix. Put on a lid, and leave it in the fridge for 24 hours.

Dough: Pour the starter into the mixing bowl. Add the egg yolks and the low-fat milk, and mix thoroughly using the mixer.

Sift the flour, sugar, and salt into another bowl. Rub in the yeast. Add this mix to the starter in the mixing bowl, and set the mixer to run for 3 minutes at low speed. The dough should now be sticky and soft.

Soften the butter, and add this and the oil to the dough. Mix thoroughly. Let the dough rest in the mixing bowl for 10 minutes, then mix again for 4 minutes at medium speed. Cover the dough, and let it rest in the fridge for 30 minutes.

Cut the cooled dough into 85-g pieces. Flour your hands, then quickly roll each piece into a small ball, and place them on a sheet pan lined with parchment paper. Now moisten your hands, and press down with your palms to flatten them until they are approximately 5 inches across. Let the buns proof at 64 to 72°F for 1½ to 2 hours.

Preheat the oven to 440°F.

Mix the ingredients for brushing. Prior to brushing the buns, gently flatten them again with moist palms. Then generously mist the oven with water, and place the brushed buns in the center of the oven. Bake them for 7 minutes. Remove from the oven, brush again with the egg mix, and decorate, for example, with sesame seeds. Put the buns back in the oven, and bake for approximately 7 minutes more, or until they have turned a light golden color.

Prosse Cake is a tradition from Funen, in the center of Denmark, which has found its way onto Als, our little island in the south. What the peculiar word "prosse" means nobody seems to know, but to this day it is a very popular cake in Funen. Many a visitor from there has dropped in on us to buy barley flakes, for making either pear porridge or prosse cake. Prosse cake reminds me of childhood Christmases in the countryside. Wonderful, spicy, and great with syrup.

PROSSE CAKE FROM FUNEN

Equipment: 8 x 10-inch loaf pan

Starter:
1,000 g boiling milk
125 g rolled oats
125 g barley flakes

Dough:
All of the starter
2 large eggs
75 g sugar
3 g (approx. ½ tsp) salt
1 tsp ground cinnamon
1 tsp ground cardamom
60 g raisins
Optional: finely grated lemon zest
(not quite traditional, but it suits the cake)
Bread crumbs for sprinkling

Pour boiling milk over the rolled oats and barley flakes. Mix thoroughly, cover, and leave at room temperature until the next day.

Preheat the oven to 350°F.

Beat the eggs, then mix them into your oat/barley porridge. Now add the sugar, salt, cinnamon, cardamom, raisins, and lemon zest, and mix thoroughly.

Thoroughly grease the loaf pan with butter, then sprinkle with fine bread crumbs. Spoon the mixture evenly into the pan. Once smooth and settled, sprinkle the top with bread crumbs.

Bake the prosse cake for 1½ to 1¾ hours, then allow to cool in the pan.

Prior to serving, slice the prosse cake and fry the slices in butter or fat. Serve them warm and drizzled with dark beet syrup or maple syrup.

BAKING WITH BAKING POWDER

Yeast is not the only thing that can make a dough rise. Baking powder is a quick and efficient raising agent. The main ingredient in our organic baking powder (made by Agrano, from Germany) is an extract of concentrated grape juice. The other two ingredients are cornstarch and soda. The cornstarch is added just to keep the grape juice extract and the soda dry until use.

The reason baking powder can be used as a raising agent is that when it comes into contact with moisture—such as that in dough—the soda, an alkali, reacts with the acid in the grape juice extract, thus creating carbon dioxide. This carbon dioxide is captured in the dough in little air bubbles, making your loaf or pastry rise.

Our organic baking powder contains no phosphate, unlike nonorganic baking powder. Phosphate may add an odd taste of "chemicals" to the finished bread or pastry, and some people also experience heartburn.

Our organic baking powder also contains no gluten and is thus suitable for people suffering from gluten allergies.

QUICK RYE BREAD

Equipment: 0.4-gallon (1½-liter) loaf pan

It sometimes happens that I run out of home-baked sourdough rye bread. That doesn't mean I have to buy bread from the bakery, however . . . this bread, made with baking powder, gives me a replacement that's super easy and very quick to make.

150 g sifted wheat or spelt flour
110 g whole-wheat or whole-spelt flour
75 g sifted rye flour
100 g whole-rye flour
30 g cracked rye
30 g cracked wheat
30 g sesame seeds
30 g flax seeds
10 g salt
10 g (approx. 2 tsp) baking powder
300 g buttermilk
200 g water
60 g (approx. 2 tbsp) malt syrup

Decoration:
Sesame seeds and flax seeds

Preheat the oven to 350°F, regular heat.

Mix all dry ingredients; add the buttermilk, water, and syrup, and mix or beat the dough thoroughly.

Pour the dough into the greased pan. Smooth the surface, score it, then decorate with some sesame seeds and flax seeds. Place the pan on the second shelf up, and bake the bread for 1¼ to 1½ hours.

Immediately take the loaf out of the pan, let it cool a little on a wire rack, then wrap it in a cloth. Let the loaf cool completely before slicing.

There are two indispensable women who work at the mill, both called Ulla: Ulla1 and Ulla2. Ulla1 is the daughter of Villy, the former village blacksmith, whose father, Christian, was blacksmith before him. Old Christian forged gates and pavilions for the garden at Skærtoft, and he once gave me a cutting from his fig tree. This has grown to be a grand tree by the south wall of the mill, which provides us every year with luscious figs. Villy has inherited his father's green thumb but also has a special flair for beekeeping, which is why we always have honey—the best of its kind—for our bread.

HONEY BREAD

Makes 2 loaves

200 g honey
200 g walnuts
400 g pastry flour
125 g whole-wheat flour
20 g (approx. 4 tsp) baking powder
Approx. 275 g water
10 g salt

Preheat the oven to 390°F. Line a sheet pan with parchment paper.

Gently warm the honey until liquid.

Grind 100 g of walnuts using a mortar and pestle, and coarsely chop the remaining 100 g of walnuts.

Mix the two types of flour thoroughly with the baking powder. Add the walnuts, water, and salt, and make the dough come together quickly. Divide it into two, shape each half into a ball, then pat them into flat discs, approximately 2 inches high and 15 inches across.

Sprinkle the loaves with a little whole wheat, then place them on the sheet pan. Using a metal cutter or a knife, press down on the loaves to make a cross, without cutting all the way through the dough. Place the pan on the second shelf up, and bake for 30 to 40 minutes.

This bread is one of my favorites for a nice summer evening in the yard—served just as it is, with a glass of wine and a bowl of olives. The recipe landed with us via Irene Gramkow, who told us that one of her friends had given it to her and that this friend had got it from another friend. Since then I've found a similar recipe in a French baking book, this time from the famous baker Lionel Poilâne from Paris. But we still call it "Irene's Olive Bread."

IRENE'S OLIVE BREAD

Equipment: 0.4-gallon (1½-liter) baking pan

200 g pastry flour
10 g (2 tsp) baking powder
3 large eggs
50 g olive oil
80 g dry white wine
150 g ham or good, low-fat bacon, cubed
20–25 green olives (pitted)
20–25 black olives (pitted)
100 g grated cheese, for example, Gruyère
5 g salt (only necessary if the ham is unsalted)

Sift the flour and baking powder, then stir in the eggs, oil, and white wine little by little. Fold the ham, olives, and cheese into the dough, and pour it into the greased pan.

Preheat the oven to 360°F.

Place the pan on a sheet pan in the center of the oven, and bake for 35 to 45 minutes, until the bread is golden and there is no sticky dough when pricked with a toothpick.

Leave to cool in the pan for 5 to 10 minutes, then turn out onto a wire rack. Slice the loaf once it has cooled down completely.

HONEY CAKE
FROM CHRISTIANSFELD

Equipment: 8 x 12-inch loaf pan

When the German Moravian Brethren founded the town of Christiansfeld in Southern Jutland in 1773, one of their first initiatives, supported by the Danish royals, was to build a bakery specializing in spiced cakes, cookies, and "honey hearts"—these little heart-shaped cakes. Honey hearts from Christiansfeld quickly became very popular, and for many years they even gathered their own romantic tradition. A young couple who wished to be engaged would bring a honey heart to their priest, who would then break it and give each young lover half of the heart, thereby blessing the union. Classic honey hearts are beautiful to look at but can be a little dry. This particular variety of honey cake from the Brethrens' town, however, is succulent, spicy, and sweet.

1 whole large egg
3 egg yolks from large eggs
100 g light cane sugar
225 g liquid honey (or lightly warmed solid honey)
25 g candied, chopped orange zest
250 g pastry flour
5 g (approx. 1 tsp) baking powder
1 tsp ground cloves
1 tsp ground ginger
3 egg whites from large eggs

Filling:
Apricot jam

Topping:
Dark chocolate

Preheat the oven to 300°F.

Whip the egg, egg yolks, sugar, and honey to a thick, airy foam, and stir in the finely chopped orange zest. Sift the flour, baking powder, and spices into the egg mix, and blend everything thoroughly. Beat the egg whites until stiff, then fold them gently into the dough.

Pour the dough into a loaf pan, and smooth the surface. Place the pan in the center of the oven, and bake for 40 to 45 minutes. Remove from oven.

Leave the honey cake in the pan until it has cooled completely. Then take it out, divide it in half, and sandwich it together again using apricot jam for the filling. Decorate with chocolate topping. The cake is at its best if left to settle for some time prior to serving.

We are lucky enough to own a piece of meadow in a place called Fjordmosen—"Fjord Marshes"—which lies between Nørreskoven, the largest forest on Als, and the sea. We are not the only ones who treasure this area. The Danish EPA collects seed samples from the meadows to trace indigenous plants, because it considers Fjordmosen to be an area of unspoiled beauty containing rare and endangered plants. I love to take my dog there for brisk walks and to picnic with my family on beautiful summer days with coffee and cake.

PICNIC MUFFINS

Makes 12 muffins
Equipment: muffin cups or homemade baking parchment cups

300 g pastry flour
10 g (approx. 2½ tsp) baking powder
3 g fine salt
3 g ground pepper
2 large eggs
200 g whole milk
150 g grated zucchini
150 g grated cheese; for example, cheddar
3 finely chopped scallions or some finely cut chives

Preheat the oven to 360°F.

Sift the flour and baking powder into the bowl. Add the salt and pepper. Beat the eggs and milk, and pour into the flour. Mix thoroughly until homogeneous. Now fold the zucchini, cheese, and scallions into the dough.

Distribute the dough into 12 muffin cups or home-made parchment cups. Place the cups on a sheet pan in the center of the oven, and bake the little cakes for 30 to 35 minutes, until they are a lovely golden color and there is no sticky dough when pricked with a toothpick.

Elderflowers grow in abundance in the many hedgerows that surround the fields at Skærtoft. There are so many that we can't use them all, even though we make lemonade, batter and fry the flowers, and make soup and juice from the black elderberries picked in the autumn. These little muffinlike pastries are one of the newer recipes in my elderflower repertoire, but there is no doubt that they will become a Skærtoft summer classic for our afternoon coffees.

ELDERFLOWER MUFFINS WITH MASCARPONE

Makes 10 to 12 muffins
Equipment: paper muffin cups

110 g soft, unsalted butter
110 g light cane sugar
50 g almond flour
2 eggs
60 g elderflower concentrate
75 g pastry flour
10 g (approx. 2 tsp) baking powder

Glaze:
200 g mascarpone cheese
100 g sour cream
45 g elderflower concentrate
90 g icing sugar

Decoration:
Fresh elderflowers, rinsed and patted dry

Preheat the oven to 360°F.

Whip the butter and cane sugar until full of air. Add the almond flour, eggs, and 1 tbsp of elderflower concentrate. Mix thoroughly. Sift the flour and baking powder into the dough, and blend it all quickly.

Divide the dough into muffin cups. Place on a sheet pan, and load into the center of the oven. Bake the cakes for around 20 minutes, until they are lightly golden.

Leave the finished cakes in the muffin cups. Prick the muffins while still warm and drizzle with the remaining elderflower concentrate.

Whip the mascarpone, sour cream, elderflower concentrate, and icing sugar to a soft cream. When the cakes have cooled completely, spread a teaspoon of icing onto each muffin, and decorate with elderflowers.

Coffee and cake in the same mouthful: That's what this little brownie-inspired cake tastes like. I picked up the recipe in Germany, just across the border, from an acquaintance who loves coffee and cake as much as we do. She calls the cake a brownie . . . but I found I missed the chocolate, so I chose to call it a cappuccino cake instead. It's no less delicious, though!

CAPPUCCINO CAKES

Makes 25 to 28 pieces
Equipment: mixer, 8 x 12-inch baking pan

240 g pastry flour
10 g (approx. 2 tsp) baking powder
4 g (approx. 1 tsp) pure cocoa powder
225 g soft, unsalted butter
220 g light cane sugar
4 large eggs, beaten
25 g (approx. 2 tbsp) very strong brewed organic coffee

Icing:
120 g white chocolate broken into pieces
60 g soft, unsalted butter
45 g (approx. 3½ tbsp) milk
230 g icing sugar

Decoration:
A little pure cocoa powder for dusting

Preheat the oven to 360°F. Butter the baking pan, or line with parchment paper.

Sift the flour, baking powder, and pure cocoa powder into the bowl. Add the butter, sugar, beaten eggs, and coffee. Stir or whip thoroughly using your electric mixer until the dough is fluffy and shiny. Pour it into the pan, and smooth the surface.

Place the pan on a sheet pan in the center of the oven, and bake for 35 to 50 minutes.

When the cake is done, let it rest in the pan for 10 minutes, then transfer onto a wire rack. Remove the parchment paper and cool completely.

Icing: Melt the chocolate, butter, and milk in a water bath while stirring continuously. Remove it from the heat, add the icing sugar, and let it cool before pouring it onto the cake. Sprinkle the surface lightly with cocoa powder, and cut the cake into bite-size squares.

The writer Marcel Proust immortalized the madeleine cake in what is considered his most famous scene: The narrator is served tea at his aunt Léonie's, along with plump little scallop-shaped cakes. The moment the warming tea meets the cake in his mouth, a shiver runs through him:

"An exquisite pleasure had invaded my senses . . . and at once the vicissitudes of life had become indifferent to me, its disasters innocuous, its brevity illusory—this new sensation having had on me the effect that love has of filling me with a precious essence; or rather, this essence was not in me, it was me."

A spoonful of tea and a morsel of cake, and Proust was "in search of lost time"!

MADELEINES

Makes 35 to 40 madeleines
Equipment: madeleine pans

200 g butter
4 whole eggs
250 g icing sugar
Seeds from 1 vanilla pod
4 egg yolks
30 g (approx. 2 tbsp) lemon juice
Grated zest of 1 lemon
A pinch of salt
40 g (approx. 2 tbsp) finely chopped preserved ginger
20 g (approx. 2 tbsp) acacia honey
250 g pastry flour
10 g (approx. 2 tsp) baking powder

First clarify the butter by melting it and pouring off the pure liquid. Use the clarified butter for the dough and the impurities from the bottom of the pot for greasing the madeleine pans.

Whip the eggs, sugar, and vanilla seeds until the mix is light and foamy, then mix in the clarified butter, lemon juice and zest, salt, ginger, and honey.

Sift the pastry flour and baking powder into the egg mixture. Turn everything quickly to form a light and airy dough. Cover it with a cloth, and let it rest for 1 hour.

Preheat the oven to 355°F. Butter the madeleine pans thoroughly, and fill them up with dough. Bake them on a sheet pan in the center of the oven for approximately 15 minutes, until they turn a beautiful golden color.

The word "digestive" means "good for the digestion"... so digestives are notionally a healthy thing, although in fact they contain both butter and sugar. On the plus side they are made with whole-grain flour... but this wasn't actually the reason they were originally marketed as digestive aids by their inventors. Rather, it was the fact that they contain soda, which, as many people know, helps with excess stomach acid. McVitie's in Scotland produced the very first digestives in 1892. A number-crunching nerd has calculated that around 52 digestives are consumed every second in the UK today. No doubt only very, very few of those are home baked—despite the fact that it is actually quite simple to make them yourself.

DIGESTIVES

Makes 25 digestives
Equipment: cookie cutter

250 g whole-wheat flour
5 g (approx. 1 tsp) baking powder
50 g sugar
3 g (approx. ½ tsp) salt
120 g unsalted butter
1 egg

Preheat the oven to 390°F.

Sift the flour and the baking powder into a bowl, then mix in the sugar and the salt. Cube the cold butter, and rub it quickly into the flour mix. Add the egg, and knead until you have a smooth dough.

Wrap the dough in plastic wrap, and leave it in the fridge for 30 to 60 minutes.

Flour your work surface. Roll out the dough until it is approximately 0.1 inch thick. Cut out the digestives with a cookie cutter, and place them on a sheet pan lined with parchment paper. Prick with a fork, then brush with a little water.

Bake them in the center of the oven for 10 to 12 minutes, until they are lightly golden.

Cool the digestives completely, and store them in an airtight cookie jar.

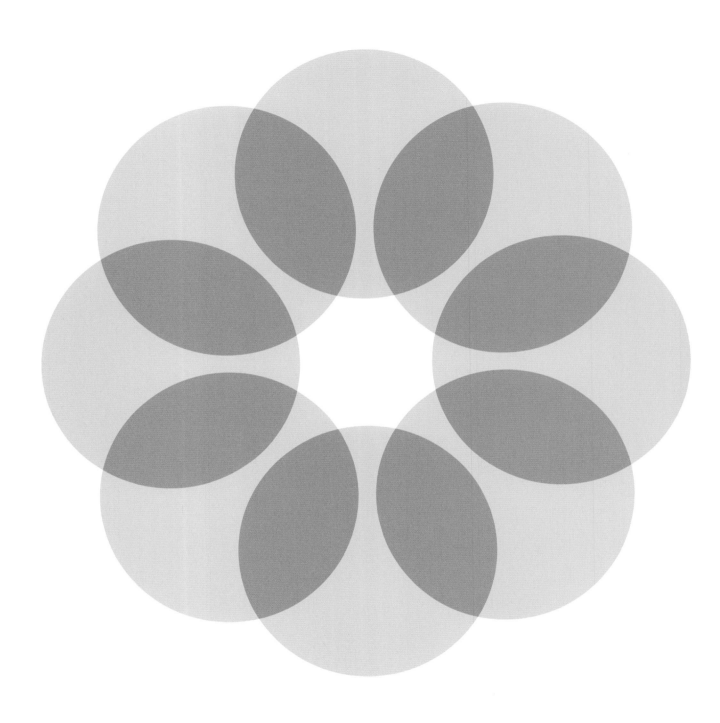

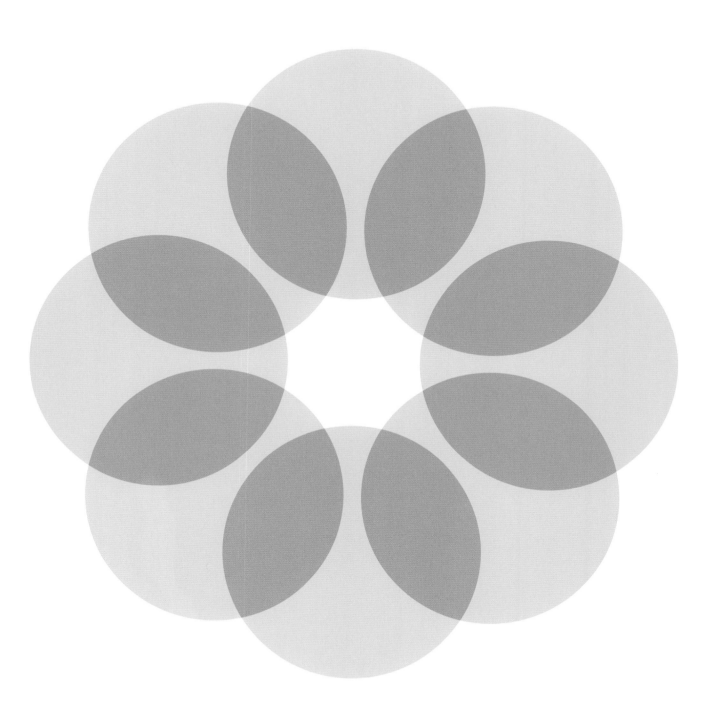

BAKING WITHOUT
A RAISING AGENT

For our courses at Skærtoft's Stable Kitchen, we have often served this special cheese pie as part of lunch. Happily, the recipe has been demanded every bit as often by the course participants, and so we must include it here. The tangy blue cheese, the bitterness of the rye, the roundness and softness of the rest of the filling . . . they make this served-warm pie a real delicacy.

CHEESE PIE WITH PEARL RYE

Makes 2 pies
Equipment: pie dishes, approx. 9 inches across

200 g butter
350 g pastry flour
50 g whole-rye flour
2 eggs
3 g (approx. 1 tsp) fine salt
3-5 tbsp cold water

Filling:
30 g dry pearl rye
300 g blue cheese
500 g heavy cream
6 egg yolks
Freshly ground pepper

Rub the butter into the flour. Beat the eggs lightly together with the salt and water, and add them to the flour. Bring the mixture together quickly, adding a little more water if necessary. Shape the pastry into a ball, wrap it up in plastic wrap, and let it rest in a cool place for 30 minutes.

Preheat the oven to 390°F, regular heat.

Roll out the pastry, then neatly line the dishes—both sides and bases—having greased them well with butter beforehand. The pastry should reach to the tops of the dishes. Leave to rest for 30 minutes. Prick the pastry bases several times with a fork. Bake for approx. 25 minutes. If the dishes cannot fit side by side, the pie bases can be baked on two sheet pans, using a fan oven at only 365°F. The edges of the pastry can be covered around with aluminum foil to avoid excessive browning.

Parboil the pearl rye for approximately 5 minutes, to soften. Drain, and pat dry with paper towel. Leave to cool.

Blend the blue cheese, heavy cream, pepper, and egg yolks. Divide the mixture between the pie bases, filling them both to the brim. Sprinkle the pearl rye evenly into the fillings. Bake the pies for 30 minutes at 320°F, until the tops bubble up and turn a beautiful golden brown.

For many years a close friend of mine from England supplied me with recipes for good old English classics. This old-fashioned apple pie is one of her very best: spicy, sweet, and tart, with the heavy feel of autumn. The perfect pie for a warm, cozy coffee break after a brisk, cold walk . . . or as the final course of a hearty winter dinner. You must take your time to enjoy the finished pie; it appeals to all the senses.

JUNE'S ENGLISH APPLE PIE

Equipment: pie dish, approx. 10 inches across

300 g pastry flour
100 g icing sugar
200 g butter
Finely grated zest of ½ lemon
1 egg yolk from a large egg
1½ tbsp cold water

Filling:
50 g light cane sugar
50 g dark brown sugar
Finely grated zest from ½ lemon
Finely grated zest from 1 orange
30 g (approx. 2 tbsp) pastry flour
1 tsp ground cinnamon
½ tsp grated nutmeg
50 g soft raisins
50 g almonds, blanched and chopped
500 g tart apples, peeled and sliced

For brushing:
1 egg beaten with a little cold water

Sift the flour and icing sugar into a mixing bowl. Rub in the butter, add the lemon zest and egg yolk, and mix thoroughly. Then add the water, and quickly bring the dough together. Wrap it in plastic wrap, and let it rest in the fridge for at least 1 hour.

Preheat the oven to 355°F.

Roll out two-thirds of the pastry, and use it to line the buttered pie dish. It should reach to the top of the dish. Roll out the rest of the pastry for use as a lid to cover the filling.

Mix the cane sugar and brown sugar thoroughly with the lemon and orange zest, flour, cinnamon, nutmeg, raisins, and almonds. Place half of the apple wedges in an even layer in the bottom of the prepared pie dish, and sprinkle with half of the filling. Then lay out another layer of apple slices and the remaining filling. Cover the pie with the pastry lid, and close it by pressing around the edges of the dish. Cut two to three small holes in the pastry lid, to allow the steam to escape during baking. Excess pastry dough may be used for decoration.

Brush the pie with egg wash before it goes into the oven.

Bake the pie for 30 to 45 minutes, until golden in color. If necessary, cover it with aluminum foil for the final part of the baking time.

Serve the pie with ice-cold whipped cream.

I have known Jens Peter Kolbeck since the early 1970s. The first time I interviewed him he had just been informed that he was to be the next official chef for the Queen of Denmark, chosen for this esteemed position because of his unique talent and his profound knowledge of French cuisine. Jens Peter is unfailingly generous with his knowledge and experience, so he has ended up "giving" me a recipe: Hanne's lemon pie. The first time he served it to me, the accompaniment was homemade ice cream with sea buckthorn, along with fresh berries and syrup from blackberries picked in the woods surrounding Gråsten Castle. My mouth starts watering just thinking about it!

HANNE'S LEMON PIE

Equipment: pie dish, 9 inches across

Lemon custard:
Pulp of 2 lemons
Zest of 1 lemon, thinly grated
100 g light cane sugar
2 whole eggs plus 2 egg yolks
225 g heavy cream

Dough:
200 g pastry flour
100 g salted butter
80 g icing sugar
1 whole egg

Blend the pulp of two lemons with the thinly grated zest of one. Add the sugar, eggs, egg yolks, and heavy cream. When all ingredients have been thoroughly blended, strain the mixture. This finely strained custard keeps well in the fridge for 4 to 5 days.

Let all the dough ingredients warm, then mix them thoroughly, and knead the dough quickly until it comes together. Wrap the dough in plastic wrap, and let it rest in the fridge for approximately 2 hours.

Flour your work surface lightly. Roll out the dough. Line the sides and bottom of the pie dish. It is important that the dough reach all the way to the top edge of the dish. Place the dish and dough in the freezer for approximately ½ hour.

Preheat the oven to 360°F.

Remove the dish from the freezer, line the dough with aluminum foil, fill it with dried beans, and bake the pie base for 25 to 30 minutes, until slightly golden but only half baked. Remove beans and foil.

Pour the lemon custard into the warm pie base until it comes to approximately 0.1 inch below the edge. Put the pie in the oven, and bake it for approximately another 25 minutes, until the custard has settled.

Let the finished pie cool a little; then serve with, for example, berries, lightly beaten whipped cream, or a soft and creamy homemade ice cream.

PS: Jens Peters comments: "If all of the pie gets finished, then you haven't baked enough!"

I was taught by a cuisinière in Marrakesh. She was a specialist in the richly traditional Berber cuisine, and the chefs' school she taught at was in the Kasbah, in a rhiad that was once a magnificent residence for a prince and his court. Prior to the late evening dinner, which was to be served under deep blue skies on a roof terrace still warm from the sun, I looked down at the inner courtyard of the rhiad. It was lined with an alley of orange trees, bursting with ripe fruit, which glittered like golden apples under the Moroccan lamplight. At the end of the alley was a fountain. The water surface had been covered in rose petals, every shade of red. At the center of the fountain bubbled a lazy column of water, accompanying the swaying movements of the rose petals with light, soft splashes. A magic moment, just before a magic dinner.

MEDALLIONS WITH ROSES

Makes approx. 15 medallions
Equipment: cookie cutter, 2 inches across

350 g pastry flour
150 g icing sugar
200 g cold unsalted butter, cubed
1 egg, beaten
Approx. 30 g (approx. 2-3 tbsp) cold water

Rose syrup:
3 cups of fresh rose petals
500 g light cane sugar
1,000 g water

Custard:
2 eggs
30 g (approx. 2 tbsp) light cane sugar
250 g milk
1 vanilla pod
10 g (approx. 2 tsp) cornstarch
100 g heavy cream, whipped

Marinade:
Rose syrup
Juice from 1 orange
Red rose petals cut into fine strips
Strawberries

Icing:
100 g icing sugar
The marinade from the strawberries

Dough: Mix the flour and sugar, and rub in the butter. Add the egg, and quickly knead the dough with the water, one tablespoon at a time, until the dough comes together. Shape it into a ball, wrap it in plastic wrap, and place in the fridge for 1 hour.

Preheat the oven to 390°F.

Roll the dough out on a lightly floured work surface. Cut out the medallion shapes, and place them on a sheet pan lined with parchment paper. Bake for 10 to 12 minutes until lightly golden.

Rose Syrup: Rinse the rose petals before putting them into a pot filled with water. Boil them until they have broken down, then strain off the liquid and pour it back into the pot. Add the sugar, and let the syrup simmer at a low heat, until it sticks to the sides or reaches your preferred texture.

Custard: Split the vanilla pod, scrape out the seeds, add both pod and seeds to the milk and bring it to boil. Beat the eggs with sugar and cornstarch. Remove the vanilla pod from the warm milk, then pour the milk into the egg mix. Whisk thoroughly before pouring the custard back into the pot. Heat it, and keep whisking until it thickens. Let it cool completely, then add the lightly beaten whipped cream.

Marinade: Mix equal amounts of rose syrup and orange juice. Add the finely cut rose petals and the strawberries, cut into quarters, and let them soak for 1 hour.

Icing: Mix up the icing; it should be set but spreadable. Ice half of the medallions (these will be the tops of the cookies), then spread some custard, followed by marinated berries and rose petals, onto the other half. Put the medallion halves together and decorate, for example, with rose petals or, as here, with a tiny flower of wild strawberry.

CHOCOLATE BROWNIES

Makes approx. 25 pieces
Equipment: square baking pan, 7 x 7 inches

120 g unsalted butter (plus extra for buttering the baking pan)
120 g dark chocolate, broken into pieces
150 g light cane sugar
1 pinch of salt
10 g (approx. 2 tsp) vanilla sugar
2 eggs, beaten
150 g pastry flour
10 g (approx. 2 tbsp) pure cocoa powder
90 g white chocolate, broken into pieces

Chocolate sauce:
60 g butter
220 g light cane sugar
150 g milk
200 g heavy cream
250 g grade B maple syrup
200 g dark chocolate, broken into pieces

Preheat the oven to 355°F. Butter the baking pan, or line it with parchment paper.

Melt the butter and chocolate in a water bath while stirring. Let it cool a little. Add the sugar, salt, and vanilla sugar to the mix, then add the 2 beaten eggs. Whisk thoroughly.

Sift the flour and pure cocoa powder into the mix, and whisk thoroughly. Melt the white chocolate in a water bath; cool it a little, and whisk it into the dough. Pour the dough into the pan and smooth it.

Bake the cake in the center of the oven for 35 to 45 minutes.

Let the cake settle in the pan for 10 minutes before you turn it out and remove the parchment paper.

Sauce: Warm the butter, sugar, milk, heavy cream, and syrup in a pot at low heat. Stir until the sugar has dissolved. Let it come to a boil, then simmer for 10 minutes while stirring, until the sauce is the color of caramel. Remove from the heat, and stir in the chocolate until it's melted.

Cut the cake into the desired pieces, and decorate with chocolate sauce—or for real chocolate lovers, serve with the warm sauce in a bowl on the side.

Brownies are America's great gift to everyone who loves a chocolate cake. They first saw the light of day in 1893, when one of the prominent ladies of the day, Bertha Palmer, requested a dessert for ladies who were dining in the open. "Smaller than a piece of cake, and easy to carry in your picnic basket," were her wishes. Bertha got her minicake, delicious and bite-size, but it didn't receive its name until the recipe was published in 1896. Since then, the brownie has stuck with us, in many different versions and with many different toppings. But the chocolate in a genuine brownie—that's what it's all about!!

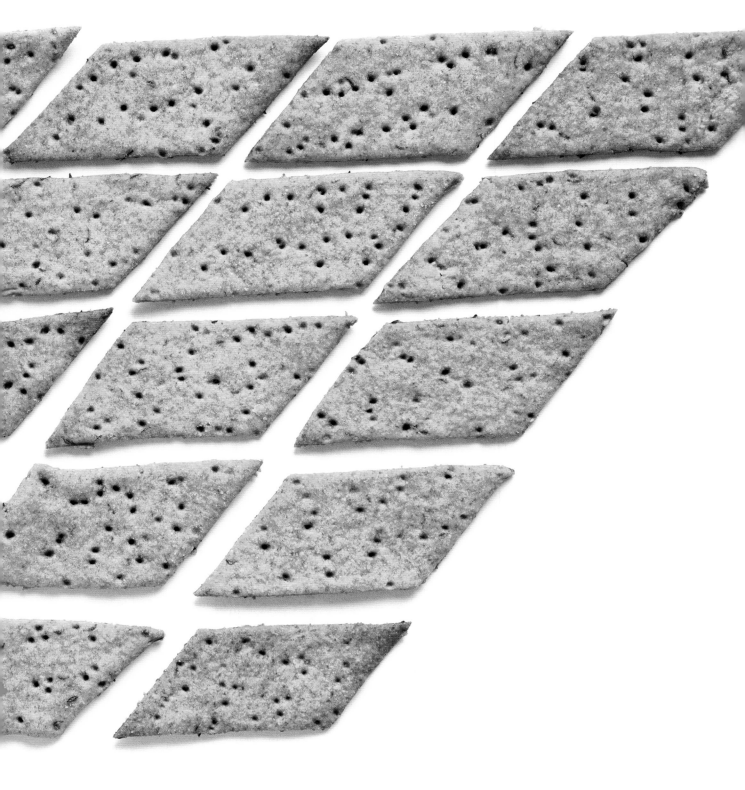

I can't overstate how much my grandson loves these rye crackers. His name is Bertram, he's seven years old, and his sensible parents make sure that he and his younger siblings, Mille Kirstine and Albert, eat good, healthy, organic food, which they love. But Bertram doesn't like rye bread, so I had to come up with an appealing alternative, containing whole-grain flour. The result was these rye crackers, which Bertram prefers with caraway seeds.

RYE CRACKERS

Makes approx. 15 crackers
Equipment: spiked roller or a fork

125 g whole-rye flour
125 g whole-wheat flour
125g butter
6 g (1 tbsp) caraway seeds (optional)
3 g (½ tsp) salt
1 tsp ammonium carbonate (subs. baking soda)
90 g water

Mix the two types of flour thoroughly; cube the butter and rub it into the flour. Add the caraway seeds, salt, and ammonium carbonate, and mix thoroughly again. Then add the water, and knead the dough until smooth and elastic. Shape it into a ball, cover it in plastic wrap, and leave it in the fridge for a minimum of 1 hour.

Preheat the oven to 390°F.

Dust the work surface, and roll out the dough as thinly as possible. Prick the surface thoroughly with a fork or spiked roller.

Cut the dough into squares or rhombus shapes (approximately 1½ x 2 inches long) or use a cookie cutter.

Place the crackers on sheet pans lined with parchment paper, and bake them (one pan at a time) on the second shelf up for 10 to 12 minutes.

When the rye crackers are done, place them immediately on a wire rack to cool.

Store them in an airtight container.

I use these fruit bars with bran for lunch boxes and long drives and to satisfy little hunger pangs, because they provide a handy blood sugar boost when levels are getting low. I find bran to be good for some extra fiber in bread and on my morning cereal. These bars contain a lot of fiber, and their robust flavor works well with the sweetness of the almonds and the dried fruits.

FRUIT BAR WITH BRAN

Makes approx. 25 bars
Equipment: baking pan, 9 x 16 inches

100 g wheat bran
50 g sunflower seeds
100 g coarsely chopped almonds
250 g butter
225 g light maple syrup
200 g light cane sugar
175 g whole-wheat flour
200 g barley flakes
75 g dried apricots
50 g dried figs
50 g dried cranberries

Preheat the oven to 360°F.

Line the baking pan with parchment paper. Toast the wheat bran, sunflower seeds, and chopped almonds lightly in a dry frying pan.

Melt the butter, syrup, and sugar in a frying pan at low temperature. Pour the bran-mix into the syrup along with the flour, barley flakes, and dried fruit, and stir until homogenous. Then pour the dough into the loaf pan, smooth the surface, and bake the cake in the center of the oven for 25 to 30 minutes.

Leave the whole pan to cool down completely before cutting the cake into appropriate-size bars.

Store the fruit bars in an airtight cookie jar.

For as long as I can remember, little Chou with cheese and bacon have been an essential treat for our guests. My mother made them in large quantities as buffet and welcome snacks. There were never any left over, and so much the better: They should always be eaten fresh. The same goes for these fritters with herbs: a French import, which I have welcomed into my Danish kitchen. Today the Chou represents tradition and the fritters renewal, when we welcome our guests at Skærtoft.

CHOU WITH CHEESE

Makes approx. 40 chou

60 g butter
125 g sifted wheat or spelt flour
250 g milk
3 large eggs
5 g (approx. 1 tsp) salt
125 g finely cubed smoked bacon,
fried and cooled
100 g finely grated cheese; for example, cheddar

Preheat the oven to 390°F.

Melt the butter at low heat, and stir in the flour.

Add the milk, and stir until the dough is smooth and lets go of the sides of the pot.

Take the pot off the heat and cool the dough. Add the eggs one at a time, mixing thoroughly. When the dough is smooth and homogenous, add the salt, cubed bacon, and grated cheese.

Using a teaspoon, place the dough in small dollops on a sheet pan lined with parchment paper, and bake in the center of the oven for approximately 25 minutes.

FRITTERS WITH HERBS

Makes approx. 25 fritters

100 g pastry flour
3 g (approx. ½ tsp) salt
20 g (approx. 1 tbsp) olive oil
1 large egg, separated into yolk and white
15 g (approx. 1 tbsp) ice cold water
15 g (approx. 4 tbsp) mixed, finely chopped
fresh herbs; for example, mint, oregano, thyme,
basil, marjoram

For frying:
0.3 gallon (1 liter) peanut oil

Sift the flour and salt into a bowl. Add the olive oil, egg yolk, and water. Mix the dough thoroughly, and let it rest under a cover for a minimum of 1 hour.

Beat the egg white until stiff. Pour two-thirds of the peanut oil into a pot, and heat it up to 350°F. The oil is ready when it makes the sulfur-free end of a wooden matchstick sizzle.

When the oil is hot, mix the chopped herbs into the dough, then gently blend in the stiffened egg white.

Shape the dough into small balls with a teaspoon. Place them in the hot oil—not too many at a time. The fritters should fry for approximately 5 minutes. Gently turn them over, halfway through. When they are a beautiful golden color, remove from the oil and place on absorbent paper towels.

Serve the fritters as soon as possible.

TRADITIONAL COOKIES

The first few years I lived at Skærtoft, Jørgen's grandmother and grandfather lived with us in their retirement. His grandfather had been king of the parish for a lifetime, but it was his grandmother who was queen of the farm. She was born at Skærtoft and had been raised with a long history of traditions, which she cared about heartwarmingly for the almost one hundred years she was alive. One of these traditions was the huge get-together for Grandfather's birthday in July. On the tables you'd find everything tradition had to offer in terms of baking, including seven different kinds of cookie. Unless every variety was present, the day was not a success! Good Advice cookies and "Knæp" cakes are some of the oldest recipes in this repertoire. And the little "Nothings" were always the last one served—because there's always room for a little bite of "nothing," right?

GOOD ADVICE

Makes approx. 25 cookies
Equipment: "Good Advice" or pizzelle iron

125 g light cane sugar
125 g cold butter, in cubes
2 eggs
1 tsp vanilla sugar
2 tsp ground cardamom
250 g pastry flour

For frying:
Bacon rind, or a little butter or oil

Crumble the sugar and butter, add the eggs, vanilla sugar, and cardamom, and finish off by stirring in the flour little by little. Shape the resulting dough into walnut-size balls. Place a ball into the center of the lower part of the iron, which has been heated on the stove. Close the iron, and bake the cookie on the stove for 2 minutes. Turn the iron over, and bake on the other side for an additional 2 minutes.

With an old-fashioned Good Advice (or pizzelle) iron, it was recommended to grease both the upper and lower parts with bacon rind between each use. A modern nonstick iron should require no more than a little butter or oil for the first couple of bakes. However, using bacon rind actually lends a lovely spiced flavor to the cakes—so I do recommend it!

Good Advice cakes should be a light-brown color and very thin and crisp. Store stacked in airtight cookie jars.

"KNÆP" CAKES

Makes 75 cookies

400 g pastry flour
50 g sifted rye flour
50 g sifted barley flour
250 g heavy cream
1 tsp ground cardamom
1 tsp salt of hartshorn
400 g cold butter, cubed
125 g sugar
Grated zest of 1 lemon

For brushing:
1 egg yolk from a large egg

Preheat the oven to 390°F.

Mix the three types of flour thoroughly. Add the remaining ingredients (except egg yolk), then quickly knead the dough. Shape it into a ball, cover it in plastic wrap, and leave it in the fridge for 30 minutes.

Roll the dough out to 0.1-inch thickness. Cut it into strips, approximately 3 x 1.5 inches, and place them on a sheet pan lined with parchment paper. Brush the cookies with egg yolk, and bake them in the center of the oven for approximately 10 minutes.

Store the Knæp cakes in an airtight cookie jar.

NOTHINGS

Makes 50 cookies
Equipment: cookie cutter, 2 inches across

250 g cold butter, cubed
375 g pastry flour
2 egg yolks from large eggs
30 g (approx. 1 tbsp) heavy cream

Decoration:
4 egg whites from large eggs
300 g light cane sugar
1-2 tsp light pickling vinegar
25 g finely chopped almonds

Preheat the oven to 390°F.

Rub the butter into the flour, add the egg yolks and heavy cream, then quickly knead the dough. Shape it into a ball, and wrap it in plastic wrap. Rest in the fridge for 30 minutes.

Roll the dough out to 0.1-inch thickness, then cut out little round cakes, and place them on a sheet pan lined with parchment paper.

Beat the egg whites stiff with the sugar, then add the vinegar and chopped almonds. Place a little meringue-like topping onto each cookie. Place the sheet pan in the center of the oven, and bake for approximately 8 minutes.

Store your Nothings in an airtight cookie jar.

LEFTOVERS

When you die, all the bread you ever wasted is weighed. If it is heavier than you, Hell is your destination.
Old Russian proverb

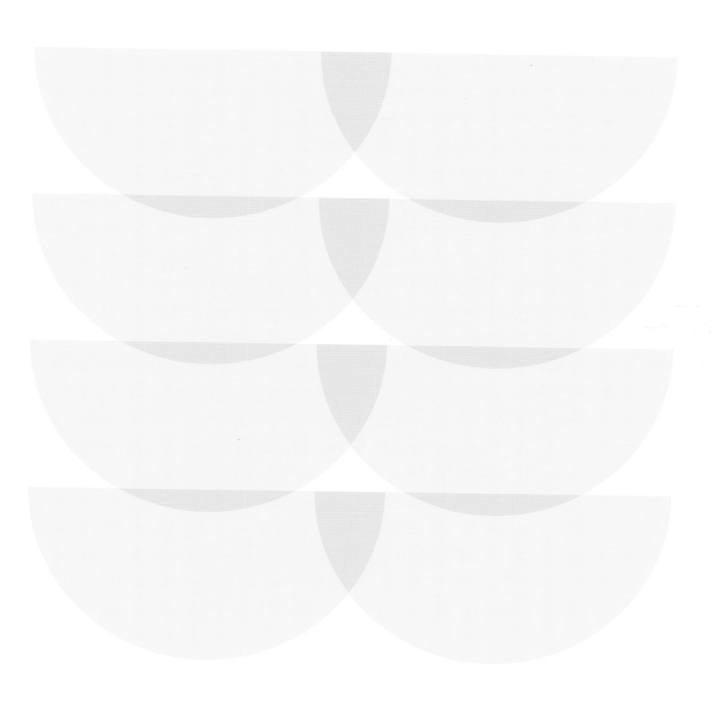

If you are really forward-thinking, you use your leftovers! Both because it is healthy common sense and because in an "old-fashioned kitchen"—going back only a few generations—you could find lots of great, delicious recipes for using up any old or stale bread. So keep and enjoy your leftover bread!

For croutons, cube leftover bread, then dry it in the oven or fry it in a pan—with or without oil; with or without spices. Bread croutons make a pleasant accompaniment for salad or soup or are good as snacks. Try turning the cubed bread in a pan with melted butter, sprinkle with cinnamon sugar, then fry until caramelized—perfect with some old-fashioned fruit-juice soup.

CAESAR SALAD WITH CRUNCHY BREAD CROUTONS

Cubed bread:
Cube day-old bread slices, then fry them in olive oil in a frying pan. When they are crunchy and golden, add a finely chopped onion, 1 clove of finely chopped garlic, oregano, thyme, pepper, and a little sea salt, and mix everything quickly. Cool croutons a little before serving.

Dressing:
1 egg yolk, pasteurized
3 anchovy filets in oil
5 g (approx. 1 tsp) Dijon mustard
30 g (approx. 2–3 tbsp) lemon juice
Salt and freshly ground pepper
80 g (approx. 4 tbsp) olive oil

For the salad:
1–2 heads Romaine lettuce
Freshly shaved Parmesan
Fried chicken breast (optional)

Make the croutons first, so they have time to cool a bit before you put them on the finished salad.

Mix the egg yolk, anchovies, Dijon mustard, lemon juice, and salt and pepper in a blender. Add the oil in a thin stream bit by bit until the dressing is smooth and thick.

Rinse and dry the lettuce; use whole leaves or chop them into appropriate-size pieces. Arrange the lettuce in a bowl, pour over the dressing, sprinkle with bread croutons and freshly shaved Parmesan, and serve.

Adding slices of fried chicken breast turns this salad into a lunch dish.

Bruschetta, just like spaghetti and pizza, mean Italy. They are perfect for appetizers, ministarters, or lunch. Plain bruschetta (bruschette, when there is more than one) are made by rubbing slices of day-old bread with a little fresh garlic, then frying them in good-quality olive oil. There are plenty of other options, though, because the slices can be topped in so many different ways. You're limited only by your imagination!

AVOCADO AND TOMATO BRUSCHETTE

Fry up slices of day-old bread in a little olive oil. Mash half an avocado, season with garlic and lemon juice, and spread onto the fried bread.

Place slices of good, sun-ripened tomatoes on the avocado, sprinkle with finely chopped shallots, and season with salt and freshly ground pepper.

Enjoy!

A long time ago rye bread porridge was something I looked forward to—not for breakfast, but as a divine dessert that I loved. It was served up in portions, with generous helpings of whipped cream in the center. I would lose myself in the aroma, drinking in the sight of that beautiful dark porridge and the part where the ice-cold cream was slowly melting, sliding into a rich brown sea. What I really anticipated was the "just-right" moment when the balance between the warm porridge, the melting cream, and the ice-cold whipped cream was perfect . . . that was the moment when I would strike, taking my first mouthful. Who said that leftovers can't be a treat?

RYE BREAD PORRIDGE WITH WHIPPED CREAM

Serves 4 to 5

500 g rye bread
700 g water
350 g nonalcoholic malt beer
2 egg yolks
75 g dark cane sugar
Juice from ½ lemon
1 tsp grated lemon zest
150 g whipped cream

Cut the bread into small cubes, and soak them in water for 24 hours. Pour the bread and water into a pot, add the beer, and cook until soft and mushy. Mix egg yolks and sugar thoroughly until fluffy. Mash the boiled rye bread through a coarse-meshed sieve. Season the porridge with the eggnog, lemon juice, and grated lemon zest.

Serve the rye bread porridge hot in warm dishes with cream, milk, or—best of all—ice-cold whipped cream.

Poor Knights of Windsor, Pain Perdu, Eggy Bread, French Toast: different names from around the world for what is known to us in Denmark as Poor Knights, a delicious dessert made from old—or older—bread. It was a favorite of my childhood and can be found today on the menu at many top restaurants that cherish traditional cooking. If you choose the best when it comes to accompaniments, it really becomes a world-class dessert . . . but it is perfect, too, for any Sunday brunch.

"POOR KNIGHTS"

Serves 4

60 g (approx. 4 tbsp) light cane sugar
2 tsp ground cinnamon
4 slices, not too thinly cut, of day-old wheat bread
100 g milk
Butter for frying

Mix the sugar and cinnamon. Soak the bread well in the milk. Shake off any excess milk, sprinkle with sugar and cinnamon, and fry the bread in a frying pan until the sugar and cinnamon start caramelizing and the "Knights" turn a lovely golden color. Serve them while they are hot, with a teaspoon of jam or fruit compote.

LUXURY KNIGHTS
Soak the bread slices in white wine or sherry, turn them in some cream, then in beaten eggs, and finally, in a mix of finely chopped almonds, sugar, and cinnamon. Fry them in butter until caramelized. Serve immediately with vanilla ice cream and fresh fruit (for example, strawberries, raspberries, or blackberries), fruit compote, or glazed cubed apples.

If your bread is still a little soft, but not really fresh enough to be eaten, then cut it into slices or cube it. Leave it in the oven at low heat until it is completely dry and crisp, then whizz it in your blender. This gives you lovely breadcrumbs for breading or for making this Danish classic, which we cherish each and every autumn when the apples are ripe.

APPLE CAKE WITH ALMOND BREAD CRUMBS

Equipment: 1 glass bowl, for serving 6 to 8 people

Applesauce:
1,000 g apples
200 g light cane sugar
Seeds from 1 vanilla pod

Bread crumb mix:
25 g butter
300 g bread crumbs
50 g light cane sugar
150 g coarsely chopped almonds

Decoration:
250 g heavy cream
Red currant or apple jelly

Peel the apples, and remove the core. Cube and rinse them, shaking off most of the water, then steam them in a pot without adding extra liquid. When they are almost tender, add the sugar and vanilla seeds, and continue to simmer for a couple of minutes. Let cool. Season with more sugar if required.

Melt the butter in a frying pan. Add the bread crumbs, turning them thoroughly in the butter. Now add the sugar and chopped almonds, and mix well. When the sugar begins to caramelize, take the pan off the heat and let it cool.

For serving: Place a layer of cold applesauce in the bottom of a beautiful glass bowl. Layer some bread crumb mix on top, then more applesauce, then bread crumb mix again, and finally applesauce. Leave to rest for half an hour. Decorate with lightly beaten heavy cream and teaspoons of red jelly.

This rye bread layer cake is a true specialty from our part of the country, the Southern part of Jutland. Once upon a time this "bread tart," as it's also called, was a popular party food and a must at the coffee and cake get-togethers that took place in the area. The fillings could vary a lot, because that was the element to which the housewives of the day could lend their own special touch, thereby creating a tradition within a tradition. In some families the bread tart is only accepted when filled with cherries; in others there simply must be grated chocolate on top. At Skærtoft we wouldn't dream of serving it without black currant jam. Otherwise, it's just not a real bread tart!

RYE BREAD LAYER CAKE

Equipment: 3 layer-cake forms, 9 inches across

100 g grated ordinary dark rye bread
100 g chopped hazelnuts
6 eggs
250 g sugar
5 g (approx. 1 tsp) baking powder

Filling:
Black currant jam
500 g heavy cream, whipped

Decoration:
50 g nuts (hazelnuts, optional for topping)

You should use fresh rye bread, not too moist, and grate it finely. This can be done with a food processor, which means that the crusts can go in, too; they add a lovely flavor. Do not chop the nuts too finely.

Separate the eggs into yolks and whites. Beat the whites until stiff. Add the sugar little by little, whipping thoroughly each time. Then add the yolks little by little, turning them thoroughly into the mix.

Mix the nuts, rye bread, and baking powder, turning it into the dough.

Preheat the oven to 430°F.

Divide dough into three cake forms. Bake them separately in the center of the oven for 12 to 13 minutes each.

Once cooled, build the layers up into a cake, with black currant jam and whipped cream as the filling.

The "Brøtåt" (Danish for "bread tart") is decorated with whipped cream; roasted, chopped hazelnuts; and/or shavings of dark chocolate.

A GUIDE TO GRAINS AND STONE-GROUND FLOUR

Spelt:

Whole-spelt flour is flour with the bran, germ, and endosperm content intact. It contains a large amount of protein and fibers and is ideal for bread baking.

Sifted spelt flour (our bread flour) is whole-grain flour with 15 to 20 percent of the bran particles removed, but the fine bran particles and the germ are retained in the flour. It has a minimum protein content of 12.5 percent and is ideal for bread baking.

Cracked spelt is whole grains that have been crushed into irregular-size pieces. Cracked spelt is very suitable for bread baking and porridge.

Pearl spelt is whole grains that have been polished; that is, the outermost layers of cellulosic bran have been removed. Pearls are excellent for cooking but can be used for bread baking as well.

Spelt flakes are whole grains that have been steamed and rolled; ideal for mueslis, porridge, and bread baking.

Wheat:

Whole-wheat flour is flour with the bran, germ, and endosperm content intact. It contains a large amount of protein and fibers and is very suitable for coarse loaves or, indeed, any baking.

Sifted wheat flour (our bread flour) is whole-grain flour without the coarser bran particles but with the fine bran particles and the germ retained in the flour. This flour has a minimum protein content of 12.5 percent and is very suitable for bread baking.

Pastry flour has a lower protein content than bread flour and is, as the name suggests, very good for cakes, pies, tarts, crackers, and so on. The fine bran particles and germ are intact in this stone-ground flour.

Cracked wheat is whole grains that have been crushed into irregular-size pieces. Cracked wheat is very suitable for bread baking and porridge.

Wheat chops are whole grains that have been cut into uniformly sized pieces. They are suitable for bread baking and also for mixes with other grains.

Wheat bran is coarse bran particles that have been removed when making the fine sifted wheat flour. Bran has a high proportion of fibers and minerals and is very suitable for bread baking, porridge, and sprinkling on yogurt.

Wheat flakes are whole grains that have been steamed and rolled; ideal for mueslis, porridge, and bread baking.

Barley:

Sifted barley flour is whole-grain flour with 25 percent of the bran particles removed. It is ideal for all types of bread and cakes made without yeast (for example, crisp bread and crackers) and for adding flavor to many types of bread. Furthermore, this flour is perfect for both Russian pancakes (blini) and "regular" ones. Barley flour is used in many traditional recipes, as shown in this book.

Finely cracked barley is whole grains that have been crushed into irregularly sized and small pieces. It is used in quite a few traditional Danish and Nordic recipes; for instance, curly kale soup, fruit soup, and fruit porridges.

Barley flakes are whole grains that have been steamed, heated up, and rolled. The resulting flakes are very good for bread baking, porridge, and mueslis.

Barley chops are whole grains that have been cut into uniformly sized pieces. They are suitable for bread baking and also for mixes with other grains.

Pearl barley is whole grains that have been polished; that is, the outermost layers of cellulosic bran have been removed. It is the Grand Old Gentleman of traditional Danish-Nordic cooking.

Rye:

Whole-rye flour is flour with the bran, germ, and endosperm content intact. It is very suitable for making rye bread and for adding flavor to bread and pastry.

Sifted rye flour is whole-grain flour with 15 to 20 percent of the bran particles removed. The fine bran particles and germ are retained in the flour.

Cracked rye consists of whole grains that have been crushed into irregular-size pieces. Cracked rye is very suitable for bread baking and porridge.

Rye chops are whole grains that have been cut into uniformly sized pieces. They are suitable for bread baking and also for mixes with other grains.

Pearl rye is whole grains that have been polished; that is, the outermost layers of cellulosic bran have been removed. Pearls are excellent for cooking but can be used for bread baking as well.

Rye flakes are whole grains that have been steamed and rolled; ideal for bread baking, porridge, and mueslis.

THANK YOU

In addition to the joys of baking and the desire for experimentation that were bestowed on me in early childhood, I was fortunate enough as an adult to have had a truly skillful bread baker as my neighbor. Elin Værge was, among many other things, the person who introduced me to the addictive pleasures of baking rye bread.

My numerous classes at the Bertinet Kitchen with French Master Baker Richard Bertinet were my quantum leap into the deeply inspiring world of professional baking, a world that embraces fascinating science, all the challenges of practical craft, and the sensual gratification of relishing good bread. I also owe the English Master Baker Andrew Whitley a big thanks for convincing me further that "bread matters"; and finally, I am in great debt to the American Master Baker Jeffrey Hamelman, whose fantastic book *Bread: A Baker's Book of Techniques and Recipes* has been an essential source of inspiration.

Two other people have inspired and challenged me—not in terms of baking, but in the very demanding discipline of putting a book together. These are Thomas Tolstrup and Pia Darfelt, photographer and graphic designer! Right from my tentative beginnings, they have been my professional partners and have, with their respective competencies, worked hard to realize my ideas. They stamped their own marks on this book in such definitive ways that it became better than I ever dreamed of.

For the English edition of the book I would like to direct a huge thank-you to Rob and Marie-Louise for having captured the feel and atmosphere of the Danish version and communicated it exquisitely to an English-speaking audience; and also to Makenna Goodman and everyone else at Chelsea Green Publishing for having the courage to publish *Home Baked* in the United States.

Most inspirational of all, however, is to be a part of the team at Skærtoft Mølle, where Jørgen, Marie-Louise, Ulla1, Ulla2, Özlem, Katrine, Inger, Ester, Kaj, Lars, Oke, and Henning are always a willing but far from uncritical test panel for my baking experiments. Their reactions toward the creations to which I've subjected them have influenced the choice of recipes in this book.

INDEX

"… sunshine, bread and spirit are owned by everyone."

Nordahl Grieg

ABOUT THE AUTHOR

Hanne Risgaard and Jørgen Bonde own the farm Skærtoft, which they took over in 1983. In 1991 they converted to organic growing methods as part-time farmers.

Hanne Risgaard's background is a long way from farming. She is a journalist with over forty years' experience in the media, in both radio and television, and has worked as a TV producer/director at two national television stations in Denmark. For many years she worked in documentaries, a job that took her to film festivals all over the world. The culmination of her career was her own two-hour radio show, which took place live once a week and ran for three years. In it she interviewed—up close and personal—people from all trades and layers of society . . . people with interesting, life-changing histories.

Jørgen Bonde is a trained farmer—and now miller—but has for many years also worked in the consulting business. He holds an MBA in education and management.

Despite how busy they were with their full-time jobs, in 2004 the couple decided to "go all the way," turning the farm's empty buildings into a mill and beginning to produce their own organic, stone-ground flour. Since then the family-run company has produced a steadily growing range of prize-winning products (prizes such as the Danish Gold Medal for best organic whole-grain flour in 2006), which both stimulate the senses and reflect modern culinary trends. The products from Skærtoft are sold mainly in quality supermarkets, as well as to restaurants and public institutions, and total production has grown from almost 90 tons in 2004 to more than 660 tons in 2010. Skærtoft now has approximately six hundred acres of mainly wheat, rye, barley, and spelt, in rotation with clovergrass.

In 2006 their daughter, Marie-Louise Risgaard (MSc agronomy), joined the company full time, working in product development, marketing, and management. In 2008 she began to teach bread baking to both amateurs and professionals in the course facilities at the farm—Skærtoft Stable Kitchen at Skærtoft. Since then more than two thousand participants from all over Denmark have joined the popular bread classes.

In 2010 Skærtoft won the Danish Design Award for their distinctive packaging design, and in 2011 Hanne's book *Home Baked* was nominated "Best Bread Book of the Year" at the Gourmand World Cookbook Awards.

Skærtoft is pronounced "scare-toft," but it is not that scary—really!

About the Foreword Author

Jeffrey Hamelman, author of the award-winning *Bread: A Baker's Book of Techniques and Recipes*, is director of the Bakery and Baking Education Center at the King Arthur Flour Company in Norwich, Vermont.

green
press
INITIATIVE

Chelsea Green Publishing is committed to preserving ancient forests and natural resources. We elected to print this title on paper containing at least 10% postconsumer recycled paper, processed chlorine-free. As a result, for this printing, we have saved:

19 Trees (40' tall and 6-8" diameter)
8,951 Gallons of Wastewater
8 million BTUs Total Energy
568 Pounds of Solid Waste
1,985 Pounds of Greenhouse Gases

Chelsea Green Publishing made this paper choice because we are a member of the Green Press Initiative, a nonprofit program dedicated to supporting authors, publishers, and suppliers in their efforts to reduce their use of fiber obtained from endangered forests. For more information, visit www.greenpressinitiative.org.

Environmental impact estimates were made using the Environmental Defense Paper Calculator. For more information visit: www.papercalculator.org.

Translated into English and adapted from the book originally published in Danish in 2009 by Gyldendal A/S, Copenhagen, as *Hjemmebagt*.

English translation by Marie-Louise Risgaard, with Robert Jonathan Whittle.

Project Manager: Hillary Gregory
Editor: Makenna Goodman
Copy Editor: Eileen M. Clawson
Proofreader: Helen Walden
English-Language Edition Page Layout: Melissa Jacobson
Photographer: Thomas Tolstrup
Design: Pia Darfelt

Printed in the United States of America
First printing July, 2012
10 9 8 7 6 5 4 3 2 1   11 12 13 14 15

Our Commitment to Green Publishing

Chelsea Green sees publishing as a tool for cultural change and ecological stewardship. We strive to align our book manufacturing practices with our editorial mission and to reduce the impact of our business enterprise in the environment. We print our books and catalogs on chlorine-free recycled paper, using vegetable-based inks whenever possible. This book may cost slightly more because we use recycled paper, and we hope you'll agree that it's worth it. Chelsea Green is a member of the Green Press Initiative (www.greenpressinitiative.org), a nonprofit coalition of publishers, manufacturers, and authors working to protect the world's endangered forests and conserve natural resources. *Home Baked* was printed on FSC®-certified paper supplied by Quad Graphics that contains 10% postconsumer recycled fiber.

Library of Congress Cataloging-in-Publication Data

Risgaard, Hanne.
 [Hjemmebagt. English]
 Home baked : Nordic recipes and techniques for organic bread and pastry / Hanne Risgaard ; foreword by Jeffrey Hamelman ; photography by Thomas Tolstrup ; translated by Marie-Louise Risgaard, with Robert Jonathan Whittle.
   pages cm
ISBN 978-1-60358-430-2 (hardback) — ISBN 978-1-60358-431-9 (ebook)
1. Bread. 2. Pastry. 3. Cooking, Scandinavian. 4. Cooking (Natural foods) I. Title.

TX769.R59213 2012
641.81'5—dc23

                          2012016849

Chelsea Green Publishing
85 North Main Street, Suite 120
White River Junction, VT 05001
(802) 295-6300
www.chelseagreen.com

Translated into English and adapted from the book originally published in Danish in 2009 by Gyldendal A/S, Copenhagen, as *Hjemmebagt*.

English translation by Marie-Louise Risgaard, with Robert Jonathan Whittle.

Project Manager: Hillary Gregory
Editor: Makenna Goodman
Copy Editor: Eileen M. Clawson
Proofreader: Helen Walden
English-Language Edition Page Layout: Melissa Jacobson
Photographer: Thomas Tolstrup
Design: Pia Darfelt

Printed in the United States of America
First printing July, 2012
10 9 8 7 6 5 4 3 2 1   11 12 13 14 15

Our Commitment to Green Publishing

Chelsea Green sees publishing as a tool for cultural change and ecological stewardship. We strive to align our book manufacturing practices with our editorial mission and to reduce the impact of our business enterprise in the environment. We print our books and catalogs on chlorine-free recycled paper, using vegetable-based inks whenever possible. This book may cost slightly more because we use recycled paper, and we hope you'll agree that it's worth it. Chelsea Green is a member of the Green Press Initiative (www.greenpressinitiative.org), a nonprofit coalition of publishers, manufacturers, and authors working to protect the world's endangered forests and conserve natural resources. *Home Baked* was printed on FSC®-certified paper supplied by Quad Graphics that contains 10% postconsumer recycled fiber.

Library of Congress Cataloging-in-Publication Data

Risgaard, Hanne.
 [Hjemmebagt. English]
 Home baked : Nordic recipes and techniques for organic bread and pastry / Hanne Risgaard ; foreword by Jeffrey Hamelman ; photography by Thomas Tolstrup ; translated by Marie-Louise Risgaard, with Robert Jonathan Whittle.
    pages cm
 ISBN 978-1-60358-430-2 (hardback) – ISBN 978-1-60358-431-9 (ebook)
 1. Bread. 2. Pastry. 3. Cooking, Scandinavian. 4. Cooking (Natural foods) I. Title.

 TX769.R59213 2012
  641.81'5–dc23
                    2012016849

Chelsea Green Publishing
85 North Main Street, Suite 120
White River Junction, VT 05001
(802) 295-6300
www.chelseagreen.com